BUSINESS MEETS THE BIBLE

CUSTOMER SERVICE:
APPLYING TIME-TESTED CONCEPTS TO YOUR PLACE OF WORK

DAVID E. REED

BUSINESS MEETS THE BIBLE

CUSTOMER SERVICE:
APPLYING TIME-TESTED CONCEPTS TO YOUR PLACE OF WORK

Inquiries regarding permission for use of the material contained in this book should be addressed to:

> Customer Centered Consulting Group, Inc.
> 5729 Lebanon Dr., Suite 144-222
> Frisco, TX 75034

Printed in the United States of America
ISBN: 0-9762493-0-8

Credits
Copy Editor   Elizabeth Young, Dallas, TX
Book design & production   Melissa Monogue, Back Porch Creative, Plano, TX

Whoever wishes to become great among
you shall be your servant.

The Son of Man did not come to be *served*,
but to *serve*, and to give His life
a ransom for many.

Matthew 20: 26, 28

TABLE OF CONTENTS

INTRODUCTION

The sun was not up yet as I made my way down the tollway in Dallas. It was the same trip I had made every day for the past 12 years. My father, Scott, and his partner, John, started the company, S & J Systems, in 1982. When I finished my college education at Texas A&M, I immediately began working for the company in the technical support division.

S & J Systems was one of the first companies to provide technical computer support for other companies who had chosen to do away with their own computer support departments. Originally, the company grew at a slow, but steady, pace by hiring new employees. It wasn't too many years before we were having a hard time keeping up with the demand for our services.

We then turned our attention to finding and acquiring smaller organizations that provided similar services. In doing this, we also expanded the menu of services we offered our clients.

In three weeks, it will be the two year anniversary of my father's death. No one was prepared for that loss, and his absence was noted by many of the company's longtime customers. Shortly after that day, I was given the huge responsibility of filling my father's shoes as President, working with my father's partner, John, who had the title of Chief Executive Officer. For almost 20 years, Scott and John ran the company, growing it to a multimillion-dollar operation with more than 2,500 employees.

This story is the account of my journey over the past 12 years. After several close friends asked for my help dealing with their career challenges, my wife, Cheri, suggested that I take some time to document the ups and downs and lessons I learned during these life changing years.

A wise old friend of mine once said, "Jim, you will be a success in life sooner if you learn from others' successes and failures. If you insist on experiencing everything yourself, you will fall short of your potential."

So, my prayer is by reading the following pages, you will avoid some of my mistakes and capitalize on some of my successes to make your life and career as fulfilling as possible.

Chapter 1

THE INTERNSHIP

*I*t was the summer of 1990 and I had just finished my third year at Texas A&M. Finals had taken everything I had in order to get through with passing grades. The previous years had been much easier! I packed up my Chevy Chevette with everything that had occupied my dorm room. (It was a very tight fit!) I was heading home to Dallas where my family had lived for three generations. We were the typical American family with two children and a dog named Ranger.

My grandparents lived less than two miles from the home my parents had built nearly 30 years ago. Every Sunday after church, we would all go to Grandpa & Grandma Baker's house and eat until you could feel every rib as you struggled to take a breath. Everyone then had a choice of taking a nap, watching sports on the television or going for a walk around the neighborhood.

Once in a while, I would get talked into taking a walk with Grandpa Bob. He had been retired for many years from a career as a banker. As we walked, he would share stories of the "good ole days" and the lessons he had learned in his long life. I can still remember the day, several years ago, when I had just graduated from high school and took one of those walks on a Sunday afternoon in June.

"Jimmy," (This was his favorite name for me. Everyone else calls me Jim, except for Dad, but I was not about to correct my grandpa.) "I remember when I first started out in business. I was a nice guy and always tried to give everyone the benefit of the doubt. If it was a customer, I gave them extra months of free credit. For many of my employees, I cut them a lot of slack when they arrived for work each day. Finally, I learned that if I was going to succeed in business, I had better start looking out for myself."

I tucked that away in the back of my young mind as I did many of his life lessons.

This particular afternoon in May was special. As I mentioned, I had just finished my final exams and was packed up heading for home. I was so excited to get there to see my family, but that was only part of the reason for my enthusiasm. My father had asked if I was interested in an internship at his company. Of course I was! After all, I was the son of the president, and everyone expected that I would run S & J Systems one day. My dad's partner, John, did not have any children.

I drove my Chevette up the driveway at 2207 Greenway Village Drive. (I was always relieved when my somewhat-tired car made it anywhere longer than a 30-mile drive.) I walked in the house and was immediately hugged by Grandma, Mom, and my little sister. My dog, Ranger, was not far behind barking and jumping on everyone.

"Where is Dad?" I asked.

"Now honey," Mom responded, "when have you ever known your father to be home before dark?"

That was true. My dad was a very hard worker, and growing up, I hardly remember a day when he made it home in time to play catch or do something with us before our traditionally late dinner.

I visited with the rest of my family in the kitchen as Mom prepared one of my favorite meals, hamburger pie. Before I knew it, I heard the familiar sound of my dad in the latest sports car driving up to the house.

"Hello Jimmy! How did those finals go? Did I get my money's worth this semester?" Dad asked in his half joking manner.

"Yes, sir. I think I did pretty well." (I knew I had at least a few weeks before my grades would arrive at the house.)

"So, Son, are you ready to start work on Monday? I have your office all prepared for you. Everyone is expecting big things from the boss' son."

"I hope I can meet your expectations, Dad," I replied feeling a bit nervous for the first time about this new job.

After dinner, I talked with Dad as Mom cleared the table and did the dishes.

We discussed the current state of the business and what challenges the S & J Systems company was dealing with this year. The company had been stable, but not growing, for some time now. I could tell Dad was a bit concerned, but he always felt that if he worked hard enough, everything would work out.

That Sunday, we went to church as we always had, sitting in the same row and socializing with the same families before and after the service. I can't remember the sermon, but I think it was about serving one another. I always enjoyed hearing those Bible stories but never discovered how they really applied to my life.

Monday morning came quickly. I was up and showered by 5:30 a.m., ready to report to my new position. Dad came down to breakfast with the paper in hand and read the business section while we ate our mini-wheats in silence.

"Ready to get going?" Dad finally asked.

"Sure. Let's go conquer the day!" I replied, trying to show some enthusiasm and mask my nervousness.

We only lived a few miles from the office. My mind was racing with questions:

"How would the other employees treat me?"

"Would I be able to do the job to my father's satisfaction?"

"How did John feel about his partner's son joining the team?"

We pulled into the parking lot and right up front to the main door, driving by large groups of employees walking in from the remote parking lot. There was a covered parking place with a sign that read:

I remember feeling a bit uncomfortable as several employees twice my age walked by us as we got out of the car; but not nearly as uncomfortable as I was when I noticed that the spot next to Dad's had my name on it.

"Dad, I don't need a reserved parking place. I'm just an intern," I complained.

"No, Son. You are not 'just an intern,' you are the son of the president," he responded.

I might have been self-conscious, but I felt that every employee in the building was watching me as I entered with my dad. We went to an elevator that had a sign on the door:

We got off the elevator and started the walk down the hall toward the corner office.

"Hello, Mr. Wilson."

"Good morning, Mr. Wilson."

"Can I get you anything, Mr. Wilson?"

Dad simply smiled and walked into his large corner office. I had been up here many times as a kid and never felt funny about it, but today, I was keenly aware of the size of the office compared to the small cubicles that housed the rest of the employees.

"Miss Lawson, could you come in here, please?" Dad pressed the box on his large mahogany desk as he summoned his executive assistant.

"Yes, Mr. Wilson. What may I get for you?" she asked, quickly making her way into the office.

"I would like you to show Jimmy around and let him know where his office will be," Dad responded coldly without even looking up from the papers on his desk.

"Yes, sir," Jenny replied.

I had met Dad's assistant, Jenny, on many occasions, but things seemed different this time. I was now an employee of the company, and she was there to help me get adjusted. She was twice my age and had enough business knowledge to run the company after her 15 years of working for Dad, but Dad did not believe that a female should ever be in a position of importance. It seemed uncomfortable at first, but I got used to it.

Jenny showed me to my office which was down the hall from Dad and in the middle of the row of managers. I had heard Dad talk about the business, but even though my degree was in computer science, I had no idea what I was doing as I started my summer internship with S & J Systems.

I was going to be working in the support center along side the manager, Larry, who had been with the company for a little over nine years. This was the area where our customers called when they had a problem or requested special assistance.

I spent the rest of the day completing the necessary paperwork and meeting most of the staff members in this area. Every now and then, members of the management team would stop by and introduce themselves. It was very obvious that they were not exactly comfortable having the boss' son around everyday.

Five o'clock came and went. Being used to the flexible schedule at college, I have to admit I was ready to relax. An hour later, Dad stopped by my office.

"Ready to call it a day, Son?" he asked.

"Sure. Give me a few minutes to finish something up and I will come by your office," I responded. (I did not have anything to complete, but I knew Dad would like that response.)

We left the office, riding by ourselves in the executive elevator and made the short walk to the car.

"How was your day, Dad?" I asked.

"It was fine. I had to deal with an angry customer, but I took care of the situation," he said. He revved up the engine of his sports car and threw it into reverse.

"What was he upset about?" I inquired.

"Well, two nights ago, we were performing a test of the client's backup and restore services on a critical server. Our analyst made a mistake and inadvertently deleted some important files."

"Oh boy! I would be upset, too. How did you take care of the problem?" I asked, not having been involved in this side of the business before. Dad had always kept his business separate from his home life, so I had never heard him talk about problems at work.

Dad smiled and responded, "We quickly pulled the backup tape from last weekend and restored the files that were missing. They will never know the difference."

"But, what if they had made important changes to those files this week?" I asked. I was somewhat concerned over Dad's casual attitude about this situation.

"I doubt they will ever notice, and if they do, they will probably place the blame on one of their own employees who works with their systems," Dad replied.

We pulled up into the driveway and walked in our house where my mom and sister were waiting in the kitchen. The family enjoyed a nice dinner together, but we never discussed the happenings at the office.

My internship lasted three months and overall, was a good experience. I had the opportunity to observe some management meetings and noticed that Dad was clearly the dominant one in the partnership. At times, I felt sorry for John as Dad would assert his opinion and leave little room for the input of others, including his partner.

The summer came to an end and I packed my things in my brand new car, a Ford Mustang, that Mom and Dad surprised me with at the end of the summer. I headed back to school for my final year, wondering if I had any option as to a future career choice. It was pretty obvious from my time at the office with Dad that he intended for me to take over his company someday.

Chapter 2

THE EARLY YEARS

My senior year at Texas A&M went by quickly, mostly due to the fact that I had met the girl who would soon become my wife. Her name was Cheri, and she had grown up in Des Moines, Iowa. She was an accounting major and we would be graduating together.

Our friends all said we made an odd looking pair: I was 6 feet 3 inches tall while she was barely 5 feet. I met her one night in the computer lab, where I had a part-time job helping students on the computer. She came in that night and looked like she was having trouble getting the PC to work. Of course, I had to offer my assistance. The rest is history, and we set a date for our wedding the summer after graduation.

Cheri got a job with one of the big accounting firms in Dallas. It felt kind of funny when she was going through the interview process her senior year and I was not. There is a part of me that wanted to see how I would have done interviewing with other companies, but my future had been decided years ago. Sometimes, I think Dad felt his succession plan was already in place the day he started S & J Systems.

The summer internship had given me a firsthand look at the real business world. I admit that I was a bit naïve prior to that first job. Dad had spent three months coaching me on his philosophy of business. I can still hear him say:

> *"Jimmy, the secret to maintaining sanity in a high-powered position like mine is to keep the different compartments of your life separate. The first time you bring work home or attempt to bring your Sunday life to work, there will be problems."*

I can still remember that first summer after starting with S & J Systems as if it were yesterday. Cheri and I were busy planning the final details of our wedding, and I was trying to make my own name at the company.

Cheri was staying with a girlfriend in town, and I was living with my parents. We had picked out our apartment but did not want either of us to live there until we were married.

"Come on, Jimmy! I have an early meeting this morning. If you aren't ready, you can take your own car," Dad hollered up the stairs.

"I'll be there in a minute. Start the car," I yelled back as I rinsed the toothpaste out of my mouth.

I jumped in the passenger seat and barely had time to fasten my seat belt before Dad was out of the driveway.

"Well, today is a big day, Son," Dad began. "Last summer, you were still a kid and only in an intern position. Now, you have graduated and are going to head up a team for me in the customer support division. I have waited for this day for a long time!"

"Me too, Dad. I'm ready to get a real paycheck like you!" I joked.

"Not so fast. You will have to earn that check and I'm not gone yet!" he responded with a laugh.

We pulled into the parking lot and straight to the front row reserved parking space. My space was next to Dad's, although it sat empty most days the first few months because I hitched a ride with Dad nearly every morning.

We rode the elevator to the top floor and walked down the hall to the normal greetings. We stopped at the door of Dad's office.

"Jimmy…"

"Dad," I interrupted, "would you mind calling me Jim?"

Dad laughed and gave me a questioning look but said, "Sure. It may take me awhile, but I'll try. You have been Jimmy for a lot of years."

"What were you going to say?" I asked.

"Oh. Come in and shut the door. I want you to keep an eye on Larry for me. I do not know what is going on with him, but his performance has been slipping lately," Dad explained.

"Have you talked to him about it?" I asked.

"No. I'm not going to be a babysitter. He has been here for almost 10 years and I did not have a problem with him until he came into my office a few months ago," Dad continued with a hint of frustration in his voice.

"What happened in your office?" I inquired, having grown to like Larry during my internship and was concerned.

"I had asked Larry to pull together some statistics from the call center. He implemented some new work processes, with my assistance, and they resulted in some significant cost savings."

"Okay, that sounds good. What was the problem?" I asked a bit puzzled.

"We had an all-company meeting in March. I presented the results as part of the meeting. I thought I mentioned that Larry had been behind many of the changes, but he felt I had grabbed all the credit," Dad explained.

"I'll see what I can find out. I'd better get going. I have a team to run," I said. I eagerly left his office and headed to mine.

That morning, I held my first staff meeting. It was a bit awkward being younger than most of the members of my team. Many of them had been working there when I was in high school.

I wanted to earn their respect and not have them follow my direction simply because of my last name. It was a difficult month. They don't have many classes in college to prepare you for the types of decisions I was about to face.

They each took a turn giving me some of their background and describing their particular jobs. I gave them the best speech I could muster with a total of two hours of work experience as a graduate.

The meeting seemed to go fine and I returned to my office. Weeks went by and I was starting to feel comfortable in my management position.

One Friday night, I was heading out of my office, eager to get home to attend a Texas Rangers game with Cheri and another couple, Alan and Laurie. We had been good friends in college and they recently moved to the north side of Dallas. We had 6:30 dinner reservations, so I was anxious to get home and start our evening.

I walked by the support center to say goodnight to the team when Tammy, one of the customer service supervisors, stopped me and informed me they had a problem with a customer. One of our smaller clients had a system failure and they needed some emergency assistance. Normally, when a situation like this occurred, the team leader would remain on-site and coordinate the service delivery.

I glanced at my watch. It was 5:45 p.m.

"Tammy, I am going to delegate this situation to you. I know you can handle it," I told her, attempting to express confidence in her ability.

"Can you stay and handle this tonight?" I asked, not really waiting to hear the answer.

"I guess. I have company in town this week, but I will call my husband and have him take them out tonight," Tammy replied.

"Great. I will check in with you after dinner," I commented as I glanced at my watch and headed for the door. "After all, it is only a small client."

I rushed out and headed home to meet Cheri for our much anticipated evening. She was already at my parent's house ready to go when I pulled in the driveway.

"Give me five minutes to freshen up and I'll be ready," I said. I gave her a quick kiss and headed up the stairs.

I had only been upstairs for two minutes when my cell phone rang. It was Tammy.

"What's up?" I asked, knowing there must be a problem.

Tammy began to explain with a hint of panic in her voice. "We are not having much luck restoring the system for Avery Accounting. It looks like the problem is bigger than we originally estimated. The client is not happy and is threatening to cancel our contract if we don't have them up and running by 6:00 a.m."

I was not happy and feeling the pressure of being squeezed between my desire to go out with Cheri and responsibility to my job. "Tammy, I'm counting on you to handle this. Give the client a call and assure them we will have them back in business by their deadline. I will give you a call in a couple of hours to see how things are going."

"But, Jim, I don't see any way we can meet that deadline," Tammy complained.

"They will get over it. And if they don't, they're only a small client anyway," I replied, getting a bit irritated.

We proceeded with our evening and had a great time with our friends. I checked in with Tammy upon returning home. They had not made much progress. "Tammy, you really let me down tonight," I scolded her on the phone.

"Sorry, but we did all we could. I was not able to get help from any of the other teams. The networking group did not reply to the page. The data recovery team was unwilling to come in after hours. The application support experts had us try a few things, and then said they would have to look at it in the morning," Tammy responded with a lot of frustration in her voice.

"I'll be in early and we can work on it then," I answered.

"What do I tell the client?" Tammy asked.

"Tell them the recovery is on schedule and we will call them at 6:00 a.m.," I instructed her. "See you at 5:00 a.m."

We ended up losing that client, and unfortunately, we then discovered they were a small subsidiary of a multinational firm we had been courting for two years. Needless to say, we never had the opportunity to provide services to them. I still remember the conversation with their CIO:

> *"Jim, we have decided not to use S & J. I have to admit, you were the leading contender until we had that problem with Avery Accounting. You really let us down, and we ended up missing a major deadline for one of our biggest clients."*

I attempted to offer an explanation, but he was not willing to listen.

The next eight years went by quickly. I continued to learn the business and Dad groomed me to take over the company. We had been one of the fastest growing companies in our industry. Then that trend began to reverse. We lost several of our key clients because of small problems in our service delivery. The more I got on our managers, more issues developed and the clients continued to go to our competition. I was surprised at how things could go south so quickly!

Chapter 3

THE BIG CHANGE

T hat was the writing on a big cake when the company gave me a small party on the anniversary of my 10th year with the company. I looked around the room and could hardly count five people who had been there the entire 10 years. Unlike the first 10 years of S & J Systems, we had experienced a lot of turnover.

Cheri and I had been married for nine years and had two children, Tony and Holly. They were great kids. Cheri did most of the raising of the two as I had been very preoccupied with S & J Systems.

Things finally stabilized, or at least the loss of customers slowed, and I was spending 60+ hours each week splitting my time between trying to figure out why we could not land new clients and dealing with personnel issues.

Following the party, Dad called me into his office. John was seated on the couch and Dad behind his desk.

"Jim, we have some news for you," Dad started as he came around his desk and stood near John.

I was a bit nervous. They both looked so serious.

"Why don't you tell him, John?" Dad prompted.

"Tell me what?" I asked, trying to hide my anxiousness.

John started to discuss a very important change, "Your dad and I have been partners for a long time. It has been a great relationship and we have all made a lot of money. I have decided it is time for me to step down in order to spend some years traveling with Sallie." (Sallie and John had been married for 40 years. They were like second parents to me.)

Dad jumped in and continued the discussion, "We feel like it is time for you to move into a more prominent role in the company. You are being promoted to Executive Vice President and will take over many of the duties John has handled for years."

"Wow! I don't know what to say," I replied, being caught off guard by this announcement. I guess I expected John to be around forever.

"We would like to make the announcement tomorrow to the rest of the company. John will be here for the next two months as he transitions his responsibilities your direction," Dad explained. "We don't even need to change the name of the company!"

In all these years, I never thought that S & J would one day stand for "Scott and Jim." "I guess that is right," I said, still in a state of shock.

John stood up and shook my hand. "Congratulations, Jim! This is a big day: Your 10-year anniversary and a major promotion. Where are you going to take us to dinner to celebrate?"

The next two months were some of the most stressful days in my life. All of a sudden, I had to learn a whole different set of responsibilities. The company was not in a growth mode, so I constantly had to make cuts to balance the budget.

I was John's shadow, watching every move and attending all of his meetings. This was the first time I noticed that John and my dad had different styles of running their portions of the company. I did not think much of it then, but the differences would become more obvious over the years to come.

The two months went by quickly. I still remember John's last day and the big party we threw for him. It was obvious by the gifts, cards and kind words spoken that John was respected and loved by all the employees.

After the company send-off, my parents, Cheri, John, Sallie and I all went out for a nice dinner. We reminisced and shared stories for hours, much to the chagrin of Cheri, who was not much for reliving the past.

I was seated next to John. At the end of the evening, everyone else was involved in conversations and John leaned over and said something I will never forget:

> *"Jim, it is your turn now. I have given it my best for 18 years. The past year I realized that my life was moving by and I had given the best years to the company. I want to spend the remaining ones with Sallie. Don't hesitate to call. I am not moving or changing my phone number! You are the son I never had and I will be available to talk or discuss anything if you want to pick up the phone or stop by after work."*

"Thanks, John. That means a lot to me. I can guarantee I will be taking you up on that!"

During the next two years, I grew into my new role. For the first few months, I would schedule weekly visits with John to get his feedback on a host of topics. Over time, the visits grew less frequent and I felt I was getting the hang of this executive stuff.

I continued to spend the large majority of my hours at the office. Cheri and the kids did their own thing most of the time, and I caught up with them when possible. I would make one out of every three Sunday mornings at our church. Cheri understood, but I could tell it was bothering her.

The stress of running a company was intense, especially now that it was only Dad and me making most of the decisions. I realized that I had become a carbon copy of my father, handling situations exactly how I had observed for many years. I had gotten pretty good at doing whatever it took to keep the customers happy. I found myself becoming very comfortable telling slight half-truths in order to cover up for a mistake made by one of my employees. The majority of my days were spent putting out fires, both with clients and employees.

It was June 21, 2002 and I was on my way into work. It was a cloudy day and it looked like rain was going to drop any minute. It was days like that when I appreciated my front row covered parking place.

Driving into the parking lot and heading toward the north end of the building, I noticed an ambulance with its lights flashing parked by the entrance. There was a lot of activity with people hurrying in and out of the building. I noticed Dad's car was in his spot as it usually was when I arrived at 7:00 a.m. (He always gave me a hard time for "sleeping in" until 5:30 a.m.)

Pulling into my spot, I jumped out of the car. "What's going on?" I frantically asked the first person I saw.

"I'm not sure, but I heard someone had a heart attack," they responded.

By the time I made it to the elevators, Jenny, Dad's assistant for almost 20 years, was there to greet me. I could tell things were not right. Panic came across my body.

"Jenny, please tell me it's not Dad!"

Jenny looked at me and I knew it was not good news.

"Jim, I found your father collapsed in his office when I arrived 30 minutes ago," Jenny said with tears in her eyes. "It does not look good."

I ran into the lobby just as they were bringing Dad down in the elevator. To my surprise, he was conscious. I had the EMTs stop long enough to exchange a few words with him.

"Jimmy," Dad whispered, barely audible. "It's yours now. If I don't make it, take care of the company and your mother."

"I will Dad," I replied as he squeezed my hand.

"We have to go," the emergency team said.

I jumped in my car and followed the ambulance to the hospital, calling Mom on the cell phone as I went.

It was the last time I would ever see my dad alive. He died in route to the hospital.

Later that week, we were joined by family and friends as we bid Dad goodbye in a traditional memorial service. The one thing that jumped out and grabbed me during the service was that almost all the comments and remembrances were related to Dad's career and his involvement with S & J Systems.

John, Dad's former partner, and his wife, Sallie, were there to pay their respects.

"Jim. I'm so sorry that Scott left us so soon. He was a good man," John told me, and he gave me a tight hug.

"Thanks, John. It was quite a shock," I responded.

"Whenever you are ready, I would like to spend some time with you. The past two years have brought some of the most significant changes in my life. If you are interested, I would love to share them with you," John offered.

"I will give you a call soon. I need your help to figure out what to do with the company," I replied.

Cheri, Mom and I returned to my parent's house and visited with family. That was the end of an era and the start of what would be a life changing year.

Chapter 4

TAKE ME OUT
TO THE BALLPARK!

I took a few days off and then made my way back to the office. I was there for about 10 minutes when the first of my senior managers made his way into my office. After sharing some nice words about my father, each one immediately began to discuss a significant client problem in their area. I listened and offered my recommended solution, and they went about their way.

A few minutes passed when the chief financial officer, Ken, knocked on my open door. "Jim, do you have a few minutes?"

I knew from the tone of his question he was not bringing good news.

"Sure, come on in," I reluctantly responded.

I was right. Ken spent the next 30 minutes reviewing a less than stellar financial report that showed a decline in net revenue in almost every service area.

After dealing with a few more problems and calming down two angry customers, I had about as much as I could handle. For years, I had known that the day would come when I would be in charge, but I did not think it would be this soon.

I called Cheri and asked if she could meet me for lunch. I needed some friendly conversation and someone with whom I could share my fears and frustrations. Cheri was one of the best listeners I had ever met.

She stopped by the office and picked me up. We went to a quiet Italian place that we had frequented during our first years of marriage.

"Thanks for coming, honey."

"Sure. I could tell you were having a rough day," Cheri responded.

"I have never felt so ill-equipped to handle something as I do taking over Dad's company," I started. "It's a mess! I guess Dad was shielding me from some of the problems and financial reports."

I continued, "We have had a steady stream of employees and customers leaving for our competition. I got word today that one of our largest clients was not planning to renew their contract when it expires next month."

"I'm afraid I don't have a lot of advice to give when it comes to solving your business problems," Cheri replied.

"Didn't you tell me that John wanted to meet with you and share something?" she asked.

"Yes. I guess I ought to give him a call. Maybe I'll see if he has time today. After all, he can't be at the ballpark this afternoon with all the rain we've had this week."

"I think that would be a great idea. John is a quiet man, but I've always trusted him," Cheri added as our ravioli arrived.

"I've realized over the past two years since his retirement that he was the one providing the calm, steady influence on the executive team," I added.

Cheri and I finished our meal and she took me back to the office. "Thanks for meeting me for lunch. I really needed to talk with someone. I'll let you know what John says and when I'll be home for dinner."

"See you tonight. Tell John hello for me," Cheri said. She gave me a kiss and got back in her car.

I returned to my office and let Jenny know that I did not want to be disturbed.

"Hello," John's wife, Sallie, answered the phone.

"Hello, Sallie. This is Jim. Is John around this afternoon?" I asked.

"He sure is. How have you been doing, Jim?" Sallie asked with concern in her voice.

"I'm hanging in there," I replied.

"We have been praying for you, Jim. I know you have a tough job ahead of you and you will miss your father," Sallie added.

"Thank you, Sallie. I could use all the prayers you can toss my way."

"I'll get John. Don't be a stranger. You know you are always welcome at our home," Sallie said. She placed the phone on the counter.

"Well, hello, Jim!" a familiar voice came across the line.

"Hello, John. I bet you didn't expect to hear from me so soon, did you?" I joked.

"I'm glad you called," John replied.

"The other day at the service, you mentioned that you had some things to share with me. I had a rough morning returning to the office and I could really use some of your wisdom," I admitted.

"Well, I don't know how much 'wisdom' I have, but I have learned a few things since leaving the company. When would you like to get together?" John responded in his normal humble manner.

"How about this afternoon?" I asked, not realizing how desperate I sounded.

"Sure," John chuckled. "I guess you really did have a bad morning!"

"I'm sorry, John. Is this really an okay time to get together?" I asked.

"Yes, that would be great. The Wranglers' game was canceled this afternoon due to all the rain," John responded.

Several years ago, a minor league ball club came to town and built a new stadium on the north side of Dallas in a suburb called Frisco. They were a fun team to watch and John got in on the ground floor with a private suite. His skybox was halfway between home plate and third base. John had gone out to the field before construction was even finished and picked the ideal location. The first base side had to deal with the bright sun for the first few innings of each evening game, but his seats were in the shade for the vast majority of the games.

"Where would you like to meet?" I asked.

"How about meeting me at the ballpark in an hour?" John responded. "Come around to the side entrance and I will meet you there."

John was old friends with the club owner, Mike, who had given John keys to get into the park even when they were closed. I was hoping John would choose that location as I also enjoyed the game of baseball and being at the ballpark.

"Let me swing by the house and get out of this suit and I will see you there in an hour," I said enthusiastically.

"Sounds great, see you there," John replied then he hung up the phone.

Cheri was surprised to see me at the house so soon. I told her I was meeting John at the ballpark. I had no idea what John was eager to share with me, but at this point, I would have listened to just about anyone who had some good advice to give.

I quickly changed clothes, gave Cheri a hug and kiss, and headed back to my car. "I'll call you when I'm on the way home. Why don't we just fix a snack for dinner? I'm still full from our pasta," I suggested.

"That sounds good to me. Have a great meeting," Cheri replied, glad to see I was following through on her suggestion.

John was waiting in his 10-year-old Lexus outside the gate.

"That car is still running?" I joked as we both got out of our cars.

"Sure is. 150,000 miles and still going strong," John replied. He gave me a hug.

John was one of the few men from whom I felt comfortable getting a big hug. I guess it was because he had always been like a father to me.

"I was glad you suggested this place. I really needed to get out of the office!" I said.

"I always enjoy coming out here, even when the team is not playing," John explained.

"How is the team doing this year?" I asked, not having kept up with the standings for the past month.

"They are getting better. They won their division last year, but started a bit slow this season. You never know when one of their star players is going to be called up to the majors. It must make it difficult to manage the team not knowing your starting lineup until the game actually begins," John explained.

We entered through the side gate and climbed the flight of stairs to John's box. I had been there one other time when John had invited my family to a game last season.

"This sure is nice!" I complimented. "I can see why you like coming out here."

Because John had signed a five-year lease, they allowed him to provide some furniture and do some decorating. Sallie had good taste and acquired all kinds of baseball memorabilia from several of John's favorite teams. There was a back room with a small kitchen and several TVs to watch the action from the comfort of the air conditioning. They had added a nice leather couch and a couple of chairs along with four barstools that lined the counter.

Outside there were two rows of seats on a balcony where the diehard baseball fans could sit and watch the game.

"Let's sit inside this afternoon," John suggested.

"Sounds good to me," I replied, taking a seat on one of the overstuffed chairs.

"Can I get you something to drink?" John asked. He was always ready to serve his guests.

"Sure, I'll take a diet cola. Do you have that new kind with lime?" I asked.

"You're in luck! That happens to be Sallie's favorite soft drink," John responded as he poured a can over a tall glass of ice.

John brought over the drinks and sat on the couch next to my chair.

"It sounds like you had a rough return to the office. Do you want to tell me about it?" John questioned.

I filled John in on the events of the morning and my lunch with Cheri. I told him that it was Cheri's idea to give him a call.

"Sounds like you needed to get away," John responded after listening to my story.

"I was also curious as to what you wanted to share with me. I've been thinking about your comments since the service," I began. "You mentioned that you have had a life changing experience since you retired."

"I have, Jim. It started soon after I stepped down at S & J Systems. I had spent most of my adult life building that business or getting ready to start the company. Your father and I were good partners. We each had something to contribute, and we seemed to resolve our differences quickly so we could get back to running the business. Once I stepped down from the company and had some time to reflect, I realized that one of the reasons we managed to stay friends while owning a company together was because I would generally let him have his way."

"There were many decisions I did not agree with, but would give in to your dad to avoid confrontation. The longer I did this, the more I grew comfortable with the arrangement," John continued.

"I thought it was always a 50/50 deal between you and Dad, but I can see how his strong personality would be difficult to argue with," I replied.

John took a long sip of his cola and continued with his story.

"About two months after I retired, Sallie and I attended a marriage conference."

I was surprised. "I thought you and Sallie had an ideal marriage. Why did you need to attend a marriage conference?"

"Oh, we do have a great marriage and have had one for over 40 years," John smiled. "This is something she always wanted to do and I never had the time when running the company. It was a conference designed specifically for older couples as they enter the retirement phase of their lives. We had always heard this was a challenging time of adjustments and many marriages suffer when they all of a sudden spend a lot of time together."

"That makes sense. Where was the conference?" I questioned.

"It was at a retreat center a few hours southwest of Dallas. It was run by a couple who used to work at a church and decided they wanted to spend the rest of their lives working to help people have better marriages," John responded, showing his enthusiasm.

"How long was the conference?" I asked.

"It was only for a weekend, but it was full of activities and great teaching," John responded.

"I can understand how that could help your marriage, but how does it relate to me and my work?" I asked.

"It was at the conference that I realized I had been living two different lives. I would attend church on Sunday and then go to work on Monday and the two would never mix. Some of my actions and the way I treated my employees were not consistent with the teaching I had just listened to, and even taken notes on, at church," John began to explain, sitting forward in his chair.

My mind was active as I remembered the many times my father had told me:

> *"Church is church, and work is work. The only way to be successful is to keep the compartments of your life separate."*

"Go on John. What else did you learn?" I asked with curiosity.

"Well, that retreat was the starting point. It really got me thinking. I came home and started reviewing my life. Retirement has a way of bringing that reflection upon you. It was after that weekend I realized I had only been dabbling in my faith," John said with a sigh.

"That is why I was really praying you would call so we could talk. I may have wasted some of the most influential years of my life, but I thought I would use the ones I have left to help someone like you get the most from your life," John said, watching my response.

John and I talked for over two hours as he shared some of his major realizations. I was interested in hearing his story, but was a bit hesitant when it came to applying it in my own life. Without coming out and saying it, John was also hinting that the way my father had conducted himself at work was not always right. His death was a bit too fresh. I felt I would be dishonoring him to talk about these topics now.

"Well, now you know what I wanted to talk about," John said as he finished sharing what had changed his life. "I know that is a lot to think about, but if you want to ask any questions or talk more about this, I am always available."

"Thanks, John. The other day, when we talked at Dad's service, I could tell there was a new sense of peace and fulfillment about you," I replied as we both stood to take our glasses to the kitchen.

"Let me think about this for a few days. I am grateful to have someone like you in my life and I am sure I will have some more questions as I attempt to run this company on my own," I said.

"Give Cheri a squeeze for me and tell your mother hello. I think she is coming over for dinner next week. You are all welcome to come. We are going to be trying out my new barbecue grill," John said, and then he gave me a hug.

"I will run it by Cheri and let you know," I replied.

We both left the suite as John locked the door. The only person left was the grounds manager moving some dirt around on the infield.

"Thanks again, John," I said as we both reached our cars and headed for home.

Chapter 5

FIRST THINGS FIRST!

I took a drive around the neighborhood and pulled up in the parking lot of S & J Systems. My initial conversation with John had given me a lot to think about. Deep down, I knew I was going to have to make some changes if I expected my business to survive. It was almost six o'clock. I decided to pull over to the side of the parking lot and watch as many of my employees made their way from the building to their cars, eager to get home to their own families.

Suddenly, I realized that my actions and the way I chose to run this company had a big impact on a lot of people, not just my employees, but also their families. I was 35 years old and running a multimillion-dollar company. They did not train me for this in college.

I gave Cheri a call and told her I was on the way home.

She had a light dinner ready for me and the kids. I listened to the activities of the day, even though my mind was still back at Wranglers stadium. Cheri could tell I was distracted. We spent some time going through our normal nighttime ritual putting the kids down.

"Would you like a cup of coffee?" Cheri asked, knowing that I needed some time with her to talk about my afternoon.

"Sure, why don't we sit on the back patio for awhile," I suggested.

When we built our home in Dallas, we added on a large patio out back, partially covered by a trellis with vines and flowers. At the beginning of our marriage, I did a lot of the cooking, but now my main contribution is on the grill. One of my dreams was realized by adding one of those large built-in grill and smoker stations. Even though we don't use it a lot in Dallas, we also put in an outdoor fireplace. It is one of our favorite places to spend time, especially when we have something to talk about.

"Well, I can tell you and John must have had a deep conversation," Cheri said as she stepped out the door with our coffee.

"John had a lot to share. We talked for several hours, but I did most of the listening. He and Sallie are really enjoying this time in their lives," I responded. We settled down on the two-seater swing.

I then told Cheri about the marriage conference and what John had shared.

"It sounds like it really made an impact on John. He has always been an honest, hard working man, but I have never thought of him as being overly religious," Cheri commented.

"As John explained it to me, it was more than just going to church or being religious. He kept talking about having a 'relationship' with Jesus. I have attended church all my life but have never heard my minister talk about something personal like that," I started to explain.

"I could tell there was something different about John the other day at your father's funeral. He was sad like the rest of us, but he seemed to have a peace with where he was in his own life," Cheri observed. "I had a girlfriend in college try to explain the same thing to me. It made sense at the time, but things got busy and I never took it seriously."

"For the first time in my life, I think I understand what I have always poked fun at with some of my 'religious' friends. The way John explained it, it seemed so simple. I have been trying to make it so complex," I told Cheri, who was obviously very interested in this conversation.

"John said that until you come to the point in your life where you accept what Jesus did when He died for our sins on the cross and invite Him to be in charge of your life, it is hard to understand things from a spiritual perspective," I continued.

Cheri and I talked for another hour and I showed her the passages in the Bible that John had gone over with me. We both decided we wanted what John had discovered and each prayed a simple prayer and asked Jesus to come into our lives. There were no fireworks or immediate changes that night, but I did feel a new calm and a hope that the future was going to be better than the past few years.

We spent another hour just talking about my dad, our family and the company.

"Well, it's time to call it a night," I finally said after two large cups of coffee. "I'm glad you brewed decaf tonight."

"Thanks for sharing about your time with John. I feel this is the start of a new chapter in our lives," Cheri commented as she gave me a long hug.

The next morning, I awoke to the alarm, which I had set 30 minutes earlier than normal. John had made a major point of telling me that for me to grow in my relationship with Jesus, I needed to spend time with Him every day. He suggested that I begin with a time of prayer and reading the Bible before I start my day. He let me borrow a book that had short stories and some recommended Bible passages for each day. It was titled *Growing Strong in the Seasons of Life* by Charles Swindoll.

I pulled myself out of bed and went to my office to start this new practice that became a habit after just a week. I actually began looking forward to this time every morning. I did not hear God speaking to me audibly, but I did start to feel Him directing my thoughts. I began to see things in a different light. Things that had never concerned me before now made me uncomfortable.

My time in the mornings helped me start being more patient with Cheri and the kids. Both Tony and Holly commented that they liked their "new" daddy. While I was enjoying a new level of relationship with Cheri and the kids, I was having a lot of problems running the company.

Cheri and I spent time talking on the patio several evenings a week. We both looked forward to that time to talk about the day and share what we had been learning in our new spiritual journey.

"Jim, it sounds like you are really struggling with some things at work. Do you think John would be able to help?" Cheri questioned.

"He did mention that he was available whenever I needed his advice. I got the impression he was trying hard not to force his opinions on me, but he definitely made himself available," I replied.

"Maybe you should give him a call tomorrow," Cheri suggested.

"You were right the first time you made that suggestion. I'll give him a call first thing tomorrow," I responded.

Cheri laughed, "Maybe you should wait until at least 8:00 a.m. You know, he is retired!"

"Good point," I agreed. "Ready to head to bed?"

"Sure. Thanks for including me in your work and listening to my opinion. It means a lot to me," Cheri said warmly.

I could hardly wait to give John a call. I arrived at the office at 7:30 a.m. as usual and must have picked up the phone five times to call John and had to hang up to wait for the proper time.

"Hello," John answered.

"Hi John, this is Jim. I hope I did not call too early," I responded.

"No, not at all. I am still an early morning person, although I do enjoy an occasional late morning. You are always safe to call after 8:00 a.m.," John said with a chuckle. "What can I do for you?"

Cheri and Sallie had talked a few times during the past several months, so John was aware of the changes going on in our lives.

"Thanks for caring enough to share your experiences with me. Cheri and I both made a decision to follow Christ. We are spending time daily reading and praying. By the way, thanks for that book. It really helps me get started," I said.

"No problem. Sallie and I are thrilled to help in any way," John responded. "How are things going at the company?"

"Well, that is what I wanted to talk to you about," I said. "A few things are starting to bother me that never did before. I wanted to know if you had some time this week to get together and chat."

"Sure do, Jim, it is up to you. What do you think about setting a regular time to meet each week? We could use my suite at the stadium. Just the two of us. We could spend the time talking about anything going on at work or home. How does that sound?" John offered.

"That would be great. When can we get started?" I replied.

"What about Friday afternoons?" John suggested. "That is a good time for me, and we could have the ladies join us after our visit for a game now and then."

"That works for me. I usually leave that time open at work and try to avoid any regular meetings on Fridays. What time should we start?" I responded.

"How about 2:00 p.m.?" John suggested. "That would give us plenty of time before dinner."

"Thanks John. I'll see you this Friday at 2:00 p.m.," I said hanging up the phone.

Chapter 6

TEAR DOWN THOSE WALLS!

Friday could not get here soon enough! I felt that my world was coming undone. Everyday I realized things I had been taught and had practiced for years would have to change. I hustled out of my office and jumped in my car on the way to Wrangler stadium.

Jenny, my assistant, was instructed to only call me if there was a real emergency.

Suddenly, my thoughts went back to my first day at college. I was excited and nervous at the same time, just like that day 15 years ago. I had never had someone I considered to be my mentor, but I had read something a few years ago saying everyone needs someone more experienced than themselves and far enough removed from their employer so they could be a sounding board and source of advice.

I rounded the corner and pulled into the stadium parking lot. John was already there and standing at the entrance speaking with his friend, Mike, the president of the ball club.

"Hello, Jim. Let me introduce you to Mike," John made the introduction as Mike and I shook hands.

"Jim and I are going to get together every week for the next month or so. Jim is responsible for running the company that his father and I started," John explained to Mike.

"Thanks for making this place available. I have enjoyed coming to the ballpark to watch the team play," I said to Mike.

"No problem. John is one of my best customers and also a good friend. Let me know if I can do anything to make your time more productive," Mike responded as he held the gate open for us to enter the stadium.

"See you later, Mike," John said. "We are going to be meeting every Friday afternoon at 2:00 p.m. if you want to stop by."

"Thanks. I may drop in some day. I have a lot of catching up to do at my office, so I'll let you two take it from here," Mike replied.

John and I walked up the stairs and entered his suite. "What can I get you to drink?" John asked as he opened his well-stocked mini fridge.

"I'll have my usual diet cola with lime," I answered.

"Do you want to meet inside or out on the balcony?" John asked.

"Why don't we start outside? It is such a beautiful day and I think we are about the only ones here," I suggested.

"Sounds great. I think the team is due back in town today, but it should be quiet for awhile. They start a five-game home stand tomorrow night," John said.

"You mentioned you were starting to see things that needed to change at work. Tell me more," John said to get our first session started.

"Do you remember in our first meeting when I commented that I had been taught to keep the different compartments of my life separate?" I asked.

"Sure do. I take it this practice is causing some problems," John replied.

"Yes it is. I read something during my morning time last week that said Jesus wants to be involved in every area of my life. Are you familiar with the short story titled *My Heart, Christ's Home*?" I asked.

"No. I can't say I've run into that one. Tell me about it," John prompted. He sat back in his seat.

"A friend at church gave it to me. This little booklet makes the comparison of your life to a home. The different rooms represent the areas of your life. There is a workroom, living room, playroom and several other rooms. The author, Robert Boyd Munger, makes the point that when we accept Jesus into our lives, we should be giving Him access to every 'room' in our home," I explained.

"That makes sense," John acknowledged.

"Do you really feel Jesus wants to be involved in my career?" I asked.

"Well, let me ask a question," John replied as most good teachers do by responding to my question with one of his own. "Where do you spend most of the hours when you are not sleeping?"

"Obviously, it has to be at the office," I responded.

"If Jesus wants to be part of your life and wants to spend time with you, does it make sense that He would ignore the area where you spend the most time?" John asked.

"Now that you put it that way, I would guess not," I answered.

John got up and pulled a book out of his bag. "Let me show you something. I had a feeling this topic might come up today, so I brought along a few resources."

"How did you know?" I asked.

"I dealt with the same question two years ago," John laughed. "Take a look at this pie graph. Each piece of the pie represents a section of your life based on the amount of time you spend, not including your sleeping time. Notice that big slice?" John asked, pointing to a section with the label "Work" beside it.

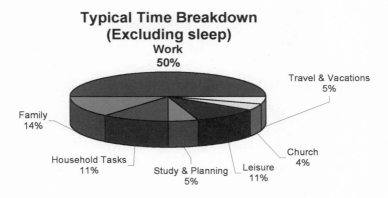

**Typical Time Breakdown
(Excluding sleep)**

John continued, "The more you study the Bible, the more you will realize it is a very practical book. It provides direction on many topics, including how we are to conduct our business. Let me give you a few examples."

"Let's look at the book of James. In the first chapter, James talks about the purpose of trials in our lives," John said. He opened his Bible and read the first part of this chapter.

> *"'Consider it all joy, my brethren, when you encounter various trials, knowing that the testing of your faith produces endurance.'"*

"This includes the trials you may be facing at work," John added. "When you have a problem in any area of your life, your first question should be, 'What is God trying to teach me?' and the second should be identifying if you could do anything differently to prevent this same problem from occurring again."

"I will try to keep that in mind when I have an angry client on the phone," I replied.

"Now, let's look at one of the verses that talks about money. Did you know the Bible references money more than almost any other subject?" John asked.

"No, I didn't realize that. I guess God knew this would be a major problem area for most people," I replied.

"That is right. Look at what it says in Matthew 6, verses 19-21," John said, and then he read the verses.

> *"Do not store up for yourselves treasures on earth, where moth and rust destroy, and where thieves break in and steal. But store up for yourselves treasures in heaven, where neither moth nor rust destroys, and where thieves do not break in or steal; for where your treasure is, there your heart will be also."*

"Jesus was not saying it is wrong to be wealthy, but He was warning if that becomes your focus, it can control your life. I think this also applies to how you spend your time," John said, explaining this to me.

"I think I understand," I responded, starting to catch on. "I think I have been so focused on growing the business and adding clients to make more money that I may have forgotten about things like integrity and quality."

"I have one more example for you. It is probably the number one customer service principle and it came from the Bible. If you successfully implement this, I guarantee your complaints from customers will decrease," John added.

"What is that?" I asked curiously.

"You have heard it called the 'Golden Rule' and it can be found in Matthew 7, verse 12,

> *'Therefore, however you want people to treat you, so treat them.'"*

John continued, "If you and the entire company can think about their actions with this verse in mind, you will have satisfied customers. Every time you personally experience poor service as a consumer, whether it is in a restaurant or buying services or products, you should immediately think, 'How would we handle a similar situation?'"

"I had never thought about the Bible as being a business instruction book, but I see your point. I've always considered it to be something we read in church on Sunday," I replied.

"It makes life a lot simpler if we don't have to always be changing our behaviors based on what piece of the pie we are in. If you are serious about following Jesus, you will use the same principles to guide every decision and response to life's situations. That is part of what gives you peace once you invite Jesus to be in control of your life," John explained.

"Alright, I have another question for you," I said, ready to move on to my next area of confusion.

"Before we continue, can I get you a refill?" John asked.

"Sure. But let me just have some water this time," I responded as we both walked inside to the small kitchen.

"This sure is a great facility, John," I complimented.

"Yes it is. They do a great job making you feel comfortable," he replied.

"Now, what was it that you wanted to tackle next?" John asked as we took our seats on the balcony.

"It deals with prayer," I started. "Prior to the last few weeks, I have to admit that my prayers were limited to ones voiced in church and desperate pleas for help. One of my morning devotionals mentioned we should pray about everything. What do you think about that?"

"Before I tell you what I think, let's look at what God has to say about this topic," John said, pulling his Bible off the table and shifting seats so we could both see the verses.

"There is a verse in the fourth chapter of Philippians that addresses this area,

> 'Be anxious for nothing, but in everything by prayer and supplication with thanksgiving let your requests be made known to God.'"

"There are many more verses dealing with prayer, and I think it is pretty obvious that God wants to have a conversation with us. He wants to be consulted when we have a decision to make, no matter how small or large it is," John explained.

"Unfortunately, most people only turn to God when things get tough. When things are going well, we feel we can handle it on our own," John continued.

"That describes my prayer habits," I said.

"How would you like it if Cheri left all the disciplining of your children to you and she got to handle all the fun parts of raising children?" John asked.

"That would not be very fair," I replied.

"Sometimes I wonder if that is not how Jesus feels about us. He is always glad to help in the tough times, but I bet He would like to be included in some positive areas of our lives as well. The more your relationship with Jesus develops, the more you will realize that He is a very valuable source of guidance," John concluded.

"What about praying for success in my business?" I asked. "My mother used to say she felt that was a selfish prayer to ask God to bless my business."

"Most people feel that way, but the scripture clearly teaches us that God wants us to be successful in our work. Keep in mind, how we define 'success' is not always how God defines it," John answered. "I have known great Christian men and women who have experienced financial hardships. Sometimes we just have to realize we don't always understand God's ways or especially His timing."

"Sometimes I feel my little concerns are not worthy of God's attention. For example, is it appropriate to pray for a new client installation to go smoothly?" I probed.

"If you truly consider Jesus to be a friend and partner in your life, I have to think He would enjoy being part of the small decisions as well as the life changing ones. Maybe He enjoys having some variety in your prayers, where every prayer is not made when we are at the end of our rope," John explained.

"I guess I should learn to turn to Jesus first and not as a last resort," I summarized.

"That is right. Involve Jesus in every area of your life and in all your decisions. I know that takes a change in thinking and it will not happen over night, but I can say I am better in that area of my life today than I was last year," John replied, taking a final drink of his cola.

"Don't limit God to the walls of the church. He is much bigger than that and wants to be part of every area of your life," John added.

It was 4:30 p.m. and the team arrived at the stadium for practice. John and I spent the next half hour finishing our discussion and watching the players take some batting practice.

"Thanks so much for meeting with me today, John. It helped answer some questions that have been bothering me this week," I said.

"Well, I'm glad I could help. I don't have all the answers. The longer I proceed in my journey, the more I realize I need to fix. The great thing is I don't have to tackle it by myself. The more I involve Jesus in different areas of my life, the more consistent I have become in the way I handle life's challenges," John said.

"Why don't you summarize what we discussed today? I think it would be fun to keep a record of our sessions, so you can look back on them some day and see how far you have come. I bought a special notebook for you to use, if you like," John explained as he handed me a bound journal with a baseball theme on the cover.

"Good idea and thank you for the notebook," I replied, appreciative of the gift.

I took a few minutes and wrote down a summary of my discussion with John. He read the notes and added a few comments.

July 5 – Meeting with John

♦ We spend more time at work than in any other area of our life. If we have invited Jesus into our lives, it makes sense that we should include Him in our careers.

♦ The Bible is a very practical book and has a lot to say about the business world and topics like money, trials and honesty.

♦ The "Golden Rule" is a great customer service model. I should think about every action and wonder if I would like to be treated that way.

♦ Prayer is an important tool. Jesus wants me to pray about my decisions at work.

"I think you got the most important points. Feel free to add to this journal during the week," John said as we stood up.

We cleaned up our glasses, locked up and headed down the stairs.

"Thanks again, John. This was very helpful. I now have something to look forward to at the end of each week," I said as John gave me one of his hugs.

"You are welcome. I enjoy the company. Tell Cheri hello and give Tony and Holly a big hug," John replied. We walked to our cars and headed for home.

Chapter 7

IT STARTS AT THE TOP

The next week was filled with more challenges at work. We were continuing to have a difficult time holding on to the good employees and several of our smaller customers switched over to our main competition.

It was Friday morning. I pulled up in the parking space reserved for me and rode the "Executives Only" elevator to my top floor office. I have to admit I was growing more and more aware of the looks I received when I got out of my car each morning. I had never really questioned it because Dad had made these things such a normal part of his position, and I easily developed the expectation that it was a perk of owning the company.

I attended a few meetings to review the details of some accounts that were moving from one team to another. We had experienced so much turnover that some of our clients had been introduced to as many as four account managers in the past 12 months. It was a frequent complaint as I met with these customers.

Several of my senior managers had gotten together and decided they would no longer be responsible for being on call on the weekends. They assigned this duty to the team leaders. It seemed ok with me, as I could not remember the last weekend when I was involved in actual client work. I worked a lot on Saturdays, but it was to review the production and financial reports and prepare for the coming week.

Cheri met me at our favorite Italian restaurant for lunch. This was a routine we had started for several months, and since I began my meetings with John, I used that time to get my thoughts together for the hours I would spend with him. Cheri was a good listener and often asked questions that helped me focus my own questions.

We had a good lunch. I said goodbye to Cheri and headed for the stadium.

The gate was open because they were going to have a game that evening. John had given me a pass to use to get into the stadium so he did not have to meet me at the gate every week.

"Hello, John?" I said as I knocked and opened the door to his suite.

"Come on in, Jim. I'm out on the balcony," John replied. "I am watching some batting practice. They have a couple of new guys. I wanted to see if they were any good."

John and I watched for a few minutes and then moved back inside.

"Can I get you the usual?" John offered.

"Sure," I replied. We settled onto the comfortable couches.

"Before we get started today, I have something I want to ask you about," I started.

"Go ahead. What's on your mind?" John inquired.

"Well, I never thought much of it, but for the past several weeks, I have begun to feel uncomfortable with a few things at the office. For starters, I feel guilty driving past all my employees every morning and pulling into my reserved front row parking place. I have noticed some less than affectionate stares as I enter the 'executives only' elevator while others are waiting for their elevator to open. Am I wrong to have those perks?" I asked.

John chuckled, "I could not have paid you to come up with a better lead into what I was planning to discuss today. Have you ever heard of a term called 'Servant Leadership'?"

"I have heard of it but have never given it much thought. How is that related to my question about the parking space or the elevator?" I asked.

"One of the keys to the success of any organization is that there are leaders in place to whom the employees can look up to as an example. Several weeks ago you mentioned you were losing some of your customers. In a day when the consumer has a lot of options to choose from in almost every product or service area, the key factor that attracts new customers and keeps your existing ones is customer service," John began.

"To answer your question about the parking space, let's see

what the Bible has to say about servanthood," John commented, pulling his Bible off the counter.

"In the book of Matthew, chapter 20, there are some verses that shed light on this topic.

> 'Jesus called them to Himself and said, 'You know that the rulers of the Gentiles lord it over them, and their great men exercise authority over them. It is not this way among you, but whoever wishes to become great among you shall be your servant, and whoever wishes to be first among you shall be your slave; just as the Son of Man did not come to be served, but to serve, and to give His life a ransom for many.'"

John continued to explain. "If there ever was someone on this earth who had the right to demand special treatment and perks, it would have been Jesus. After all, He was the Son of God. Yet these verses clearly state Jesus did not use His position to boost His ego or obtain special privileges. On the contrary, He was there to serve others."

I had never studied that part of the Bible, so that was new to me. "I guess that means if Jesus was in my position, He would not demand a front row parking space or a special elevator?" I questioned.

"I bet he would have also been the one holding the door open for others," John added. "Remember, he was the one who washed the dirty, smelly feet of his disciples during his last meal with them."

"Let's take a look at another verse," John continued, obviously excited to share some of his new found knowledge.

John turned in his Bible to Philippians 2, verses 3 and 4.

> *"Do nothing from selfishness or empty conceit, but with humility of mind regard one another as more important than yourselves; do not merely look out for your own personal interests, but also for the interests of others."*

John took a drink of his bottle of water and said, "Jim, it is amazing what an organization can accomplish when its leaders don't care who gets the credit. Your employees will work harder and stay with you longer if they know you are interested in them and their careers. You need to be willing to roll up your sleeves and help out when needed."

"Are you suggesting I spend my day doing the work of those I have hired in the various positions in my company?" I asked.

"No," John responded. "What I am talking about is an attitude issue. The questions to ask yourself are:

♦ Would I be willing to do the job I ask of others, or do I consider myself above that work?

♦ In an emergency, am I willing to roll up my sleeves and help out in any capacity?"

"One of the things I realized over the past two years was that my role as a leader in this company was where God chose to put me. I had a set of skills that He expected me to use to the best of my ability. This does not mean I was any smarter or better than any other person in the company who was performing the job God gave them," John explained.

"I think I understand what you are saying, but it is challenging

to not be proud of what I have accomplished in my career,"
I replied.

"The sooner someone realizes they have nothing in this life that
did not come from God, the sooner they will relax and let God
use their skills to accomplish His purpose. To be honest, it takes
a lot of pressure off you to constantly perform and move up in
an organization," John explained after sitting back in his chair.

I was concerned about one thing. "If my employees develop that
attitude, won't they stop working hard to achieve a promotion
or to close a new deal?"

John smiled, "That is exactly what I used to think. The truth is,
when Christians understand these principles, they should work
even harder. They realize they are accountable to a God who
expects them to utilize their talents to the fullest. There is
nothing wrong with having a desire to progress in your career,
as long as you don't step on others to get there."

John stood up and headed to the small kitchen to refill our
drinks. I remained in my chair pondering the things we had just
discussed. This was in contrast to what I had learned from my
father over the years. He had always made it very clear to
everyone that he was in charge. I wondered whether some of
our retention problems and poor performance over the past
couple of years was tied to this attitude from the executive suite.

"Come on, Jim. Let's move out to the balcony. The team is
starting a practice and I enjoy watching them," John said,
showing his childlike love for the game of baseball.

He handed me my drink and we settled into the chairs where
we had a great view of the field.

"Jim, I started thinking about my past and people I had worked for with previous companies and those leaders at S & J Systems who had produced the best results," John started.

"What did you come up with?" I asked.

"I could only think of one leader who, now that I look back on it, probably understood the leadership principles we just talked about. His name was Todd Rhodes and he was the owner of a small office supply store where I worked while I was in college. The thing I remember most was when we would receive a big shipment of new products. Normally, it was the job of me and the other floor clerks to stock the shelves and make a place for new merchandise. We often stayed after closing to clean up and stock the shelves," John reminisced.

"So what was different about Todd?" I asked.

"WATCH OUT!" John hollered as a foul ball came screaming our way and hit a chair two down from where I was sitting.

"That was a close call! Too bad I didn't have my glove," I joked as we both laughed. The player who hit the ball waved, as if to say sorry.

We sat back down and John continued, "Back to my story. When an extra large shipment arrived, Mr. Rhodes would check to see how we were doing after closing time. If we needed help, he would take off his tie and jump right in to help. The head stock person, Hannah, would still give the instructions and Mr. Rhodes would ask for his assignment just like the rest of us."

"Wasn't that awkward for Hannah?" I asked. "I don't know if I could give orders to my boss."

"It was strange the first time, but Mr. Rhodes made it very clear she was still in charge and he was just there to help. He never questioned her direction," John responded.

I could tell John was enjoying thinking about those early days in his career as he continued, "There was one more thing that stood out about Mr. Rhodes. He was excellent with our customers. He spent at least half of his day on the floor helping customers. He had a great knack of listening to them describe what they were looking for and then finding the right product to meet their needs. Many customers never knew he was the owner of the store."

"Did he ever have to deal with upset customers?" I asked, thinking about a problem we had with a customer earlier in the week. I always dreaded it when my leadership team dragged me into their problems.

"Who was it this week?" John smiled as he guessed there was a reason for my question. After two years, he still liked to hear what was going on with the clients.

I laughed and gave John a quick explanation of the problem I was thinking about.

John took a drink and said, "That was where Mr. Rhodes really shined! It did not happen often, but once in a while someone would be upset about a problem with a product or with something they misunderstood in one of our ads. Mr. Rhodes would listen calmly and before I knew it, they were both talking and had come up with a solution that was agreeable to the customer. He had a unique ability to diffuse an angry customer."

I was feeling very inadequate as a leader. "I guess I should take a more active role in dealing with our customer issues," I commented.

"Don't feel bad," John replied. "I did not do a very good job of that while I was there either. If I had to do it all over again, I would spend much less time in my office reviewing reports and more time in front of the customer."

"Jim, if you expect your staff and leadership team to deliver excellent customer service, they have to see it from you first. This includes how you treat both them and your customers. I know dealing with upset customers is not a fun part of the job, but if you demonstrate what you expect, they will model it. It all starts at the top!"

"Well, I think we have covered enough for the day," John said.

"I agree. I feel like I have been under the microscope and unfortunately, I did not pass the test," I responded.

"That is ok, Jim. Don't expect to change everything over night. That is a common feeling when you first enter into a relationship with Jesus. He will gently point out where you need to change. The good news is you are not alone. He won't ask you to change anything He is not willing to help you with. The important thing is that you are sensitive to what He is teaching you and you are making some progress every day," John said, trying to encourage me in my journey.

"I guess you want me to summarize what we talked about today?" I asked.

"You bet," John responded as he turned to face me.

I looked over my notepad where I had written down the key points for the day.

July 12 – Meeting with John

♦ *Jesus is a great model of leadership. He could have demanded the perks of His position, but He served others instead.*

♦ *Just because I am in a leadership position does not mean I am smarter or better than people in other roles. That is the position God arranged for me.*

♦ *Leaders must be willing to jump in and help when needed, instead of thinking they are above any job.*

♦ *I need to lead by example in dealing with the customers. My employees will follow my lead.*

♦ *Don't get discouraged. I don't have to change everything at once.*

"Thanks so much, John. I'm not sure I really wanted to hear everything you said today, but I know it is the right thing to do. I am going to make some changes starting tomorrow," I said as we both stood up to head back inside.

"I will be anxious to hear about it next week. Don't hesitate to call during the week if you ever need to use me as a sounding board. You don't have to wait until Friday each week to call me," John offered.

"I appreciate that, John. I'm sure there will be times when I will need a mid-week boost."

"I'm going to hang out here for awhile and watch some more of the practice. Maybe I can catch a foul ball!" John laughed. We shook hands and he gave me his traditional hug. "Tell Cheri hello for me."

"I will. See you next week," I replied as I headed down the stairs to the parking lot.

Mike, the President of the Wranglers, was making the rounds getting ready for his customers who would start arriving in the next hour.

"Hello, Jim," Mike shouted as he walked toward me after inspecting one of his food locations.

"Hi, Mike. Ready for the big game tonight?" I inquired as we shook hands.

"Sure am. The team is doing great and we have had outstanding crowds for this home stand. How are your meetings going with John?" Mike asked.

"Very well. I don't know what I would do without him. The Lord is using him to help change my life and the way I run my company," I responded.

"Glad to hear it. He is a great customer and friend. Let me know if I can ever be of any assistance," Mike offered. He continued on his walk around the stadium.

"Thanks, Mike. I will," I called out as I headed to my car. Cheri and I were going out on a date. My mom was watching the kids and we were going to have a nice dinner and then catch a movie. I planned on telling her about my meeting with John and the changes I planned to make at the office.

Chapter 8

THE FIRST STEPS

It was Saturday morning, 6:00 a.m. I awoke with all kinds of thoughts going through my mind. I quietly got out of bed and went to my study to have my morning time with the Lord. We had been out late the night before, and I knew Cheri would want to sleep a little longer.

I was so excited to head up to the office and implement several ideas I had discussed with John the day before. I had just finished spending some time reading the Bible and praying, when Cheri opened the door to my study.

"Boy, you're up early for a Saturday!" Cheri said as she smiled, knowing I had big plans for the day.

"I am going to head to the office for awhile. I'll be home by lunch and we can take the kids to that new movie, if they would like that," I said. I gave Cheri a hug and kiss and grabbed my keys.

"I don't think Tony and Holly would ever turn down going to a movie. Have fun. We will be ready to go when you get home. Do you want to go out for lunch or should we get snacks at the movie?" Cheri asked.

"You and the kids decide. I'll be home at noon," I replied.

I grabbed my toolbox, jumped in the car and headed to the office. I was genuinely excited and could not wait to put my plans into action.

As I pulled into the parking lot of S & J Systems, I looked at the sign in front of my parking space:

I got out of my car and took out my ratchet set and a wrench and took down the sign. It felt good! I continued to take down the signs for the rest of the executive team. I put the signs in my trunk and then headed inside. I left the poles as I had plans to create an Employee of the Month reserved space.

The next target was the:

elevator sign. Pulling out my screwdriver, I promptly removed the sign. I went to my office to work on a presentation I wanted to make to my leadership team first thing Monday morning. I knew they would be surprised to find their reserved parking spaces gone, so I wanted to explain this change to them personally.

I was determined it was going to be a new day at S & J Systems and it was going to begin with a change in my leadership.

Before I realized it, the time was 11:30 a.m. I knew I would have two kids waiting at the door. I packed up my tools and headed back down the newly appointed general elevator.

Just as I thought, Tony and Holly were in the front yard as I rounded the corner on Kingsride.

"Are you ready to go to the movies?" I yelled, opening the door.

"Yes. Yes. Yes," was the immediate response. We spent the afternoon together as a family having tacos for lunch and then hot buttered popcorn at the movie theater. It was a great afternoon with lots of laughs and hugs.

I can't remember ever doing that with my dad. He would spend most of his Saturdays at the office. I know he loved me, but I wanted to show my kids how much I cared about them with my time and words.

Monday morning came and I was in my office by 7:00 a.m. to greet the leadership team. I have to admit, it felt good to walk across the parking lot even though my old reserved spot was available. I wondered how long it would take before a brave employee would park there.

"Jim! Someone stole our reserved parking signs!" Jeff explained as he walked into my office. "I bet it was that help desk employee we had to terminate last week!"

At that same time, Larry and Dale joined in the excitement.

Within two minutes the entire executive team was in my office. I told them all to have a seat as I had some things to share with them.

We spent the next hour together and I explained my change of heart regarding servant leadership.

"I know many of you have been here much longer than I have. I realize that it was my dad who started many of these practices I am now doing away with, but I am convinced that if we want to change the way our company treats our customers, we have to lead by example in the way we deal with our employees," I explained, looking around the room to see expressions on the faces of my team.

Jeff was the first to speak up, "Jim, I can't say I'm excited about having to fight for a parking place in the 100 degree heat, but I feel it is the right thing to do. I have become so accustomed to the perks and privileges of leadership, I forgot that with my position comes a responsibility to lead by example."

"Thanks for your thoughts, Jeff. Do any of the rest of you have anything to say?" I asked. My eyes moved from one to another of my leaders.

"What do you want us to tell our employees?" Larry asked.

"Nothing. I want us to demonstrate this change by our actions, not our words. It will take awhile for our staff to believe this change is real. For starters, I want each of us, including myself, to take a rotation in the after-hours on call duty," I added.

"During the next six weeks, I want to meet as a team each Monday morning and talk about this new approach to leadership.

It is new to me too, so we can all work together to help each other," I informed my team.

I spent the next hour sharing what I had learned from my time with John. We talked about the need to be willing to roll up their sleeves and work with their teams. I told them that in three months, I was going to bring in someone to conduct an independent employee survey. There would be a section of questions dealing with leadership, and we would be asking for the honest feedback from their teams.

"One of the attitudes I want to change is the feeling that all the new ideas have to come from the executive suite. We need to be spending more of our time developing our staff. They are the ones closest to our customers and have great ideas on how we can improve our service. Our job is to listen to those ideas and then remove the roadblocks in order for them to better serve our customers," I continued.

"Before our meeting next Monday morning, I want each of you to hold a staff meeting for the purpose of asking for suggestions on how we can improve our customer service. As you know, we have lost a lot of customers lately and I want to reverse that trend starting today," I challenged my team. (They were probably all wondering what had gotten into me!)

I took the next few minutes to answer some questions and then sent the team out to begin their part of this change. Most of my leaders seemed to be excited about what we had just discussed. A few probably thought I had lost my marbles.

That week was a busy one. I pulled each one of my leadership in for a private meeting to see how they were doing, and to personally challenge them to make this break with a long standing style of leadership. I had one leader, Larry, who had misinterpreted what I meant by being a servant and had started performing the work for several of his staff members. We talked it through and I felt he had a better handle on it when we left my office.

I thought if I changed my leadership style, everything would immediately fall in order and the problems with out clients would go away. It took about two days to be shocked out of my fantasy with a call from an angry client. They were unhappy about being overcharged on their most recent bill.

I gave Kim a call in our accounts receivable department.

"Kim. I just got a call from a very angry client who claims we overcharged them on this month's bill. We had a consultant on-site with them for three days. The client apparently kept track of his time and when he got the bill, he realized he was being charged more hours than the consultant had worked," I explained.

Kim responded, "I'm not too surprised, Jim. The consulting managers place a lot of pressure on their staff to bill at least 35 hours each week. It has always been an accepted practice to pad the hours on a large engagement when they came up a bit short."

"How long has this been going on?" I questioned.

"I have been here for 12 years, and I remember hearing about this when I started. I know your dad knew about it and even encouraged it when we had a slow month," Kim responded cautiously.

"I see. Can you please call this client and make the adjustments he is requesting?" I asked.

"Sure. I'll get on it right now. Is there anything else I can help you with?" Kim asked.

"No. That will do it for now," I responded as we ended the call.

All of a sudden this fear came over me. I wondered how many other unethical policies and practices were in place at S & J Systems. These things never bothered me in the past, but since I started having my regular time with Jesus each morning, I have become more sensitive to doing what is right.

The rest of the week was full of challenges, but overall, I felt pretty good when I left for home Thursday night. I even saw a new employee park in my old parking space!

Chapter 9

WHEN NO ONE IS WATCHING

The clock in my office chimed 12 times. I shut down my computer and headed out of the office. The morning had gone by quickly, and I was eager to meet Cheri for our Friday lunch date.

"Hey, are you meeting anyone for lunch good looking?" I asked in the deepest voice I could muster as I snuck up behind Cheri in the parking lot of our favorite Italian restaurant.

"No one special. Do you have plans?" she inquired without even turning around.

Cheri then turned around and gave me a big hug. "I'm glad you enjoy meeting me for lunch. A lot of my girlfriends never even hear from their husbands until they walk in the door at night."

We went in and took a seat at our favorite booth. The waiter knew what we wanted to drink and had it at our table before we could open the menu.

"What are you and John going to talk about today?" Cheri asked.

"I have had several things come to my attention this week at work. It appears S & J Systems has not always conducted their business in an honest manner," I started.

Cheri jumped in, "Do you think your dad condoned this type of practice?"

"Unfortunately, I do. And now that I look back on my years there, I have to admit I knew some of this was going on, but chose to look the other way," I responded, not proud of my answer.

"So, what do you plan on asking John?" Cheri questioned.

"I need his counsel on addressing these issues. How do I make the necessary changes? Am I responsible for paying people back if we have overcharged a client or underpaid an employee?"

"That can be challenging. I will be anxious to hear what he has to say," Cheri responded as our meal arrived.

We finished our lunch and conversation, and I headed to the ballpark. I was glad our meetings were on Fridays as that was already casual day at the office.

"Anyone home?" I questioned as I opened the door to John's suite.

"Come on in," John hollered back as he came in from the balcony. "I was just enjoying the warm weather and breeze."

"I think you were enjoying a nap!" I laughed, pointing to some red marks across John's forehead from his cap.

"Okay, you caught me," John chuckled. He headed to the kitchen to fix us a drink.

"How was your week, Jim? I'm surprised I didn't hear from you."

"I almost called you, but I held off," I replied.

"You know I honestly don't mind, Jim," John responded.

"I know. Believe me, I'll be calling you next week," I said as we settled into the chairs inside.

"Tell me about your week, Jim. Did you make the changes you planned to make?" John questioned.

I told John about removing the parking and elevator signs and about the meeting I had with my leadership team.

"Wow! You were serious about what we talked about!" John said, surprised that I had the nerve to make those changes so quickly. "So, what did your leaders think of these changes?"

"It was pretty funny as they all came rushing into my office Monday morning, convinced that we had been vandalized," I explained. "I invited them in and told them about servant leadership and how I wanted to begin to change the company, starting with that group."

"How did they respond?" John asked.

"Overall, they were excited about it. I had to make a few adjustments during the week, but they are starting to catch on," I related.

"So what do you want to talk about today?" John asked, leaving the subject for this meeting up to me.

I explained to John the problem we had encountered with the billing practice.

"Did you know that was going on when you were there, John?" I asked curious as to his response.

"Unfortunately, I have to admit I did. It never bothered me at the time, but since I left the company, I have thought about that and other practices," John replied.

"I really need your help, John. How do I go about reviewing all of our policies to ensure there aren't more things like this hanging out there?" I asked.

"First of all, Jim, it will take some time. One of the cool things I have experienced since giving my life to Jesus is that He brings things to my attention as I grow in my relationship with Him. That is the job of the Holy Spirit. You will begin to be uncomfortable with things. That is the way He works," John explained.

"So, are you saying I should deal with this billing issue first because that may be what Jesus is wanting me to correct this week?" I questioned.

"I think it would be a great place to start," John replied.

"What am I supposed to do when I find we have incorrectly billed a client?" I asked, not really wanting to hear his response.

John had a normal response when we got to this point of our sessions. He reached for his Bible on the table and opened to a particular section.

"Why don't we see what God's Word has to say about this?" John suggested.

"You mean God has answers to things like billing problems?" I asked.

"The more you read God's Word, you will be surprised that it is a very practical book, both then and now," John said. "I'm sure you are familiar with the story of the tax collector, Zaccheus, found in Luke, chapter 19.

> 'When Jesus came to the place, He looked up and said to him, 'Zaccheus, hurry and come down, for today I must stay at your house.' And he hurried and came down and received Him gladly. When they saw it, they all began to grumble, saying, 'He has gone to be the guest of a man who is a sinner.'
>
> Zaccheus stopped and said to the Lord, 'Behold, Lord, half of my possessions I will give to the poor, and if I have defrauded anyone of anything, I will give back four times as much.'"

"After meeting Jesus, Zaccheus was compelled to go and make things right with those he had cheated. I believe that S & J Systems should do the same. How you repay your customers is up to you, but this can't be ignored now that it has come to your attention," John summarized.

"But that will cost a lot of money!" I tossed out. "Most of our clients have never suspected that we would ever do something like this. Won't it spoil our reputation with them if they are informed of our over billing?"

"There is always a chance you might lose a few clients, but I think there is an even better chance that they will respect your integrity and desire to do what is right. Bottom line, when you agree to follow Christ, you are signing up for a higher standard than the rest of the business world has to follow," John explained.

"But do you know what will happen?" John questioned me.

"No. What?" I replied, not knowing where John was heading.

"The Lord will honor those who follow His principles. You may take some short-term losses as you make yourself whole with your clients, but in the long run, I believe, you will prosper. God's Word works!" John said enthusiastically.

"Do you want a refill?" John asked as he stood to refill his drink.

"Sure," I said. I stood for a minute to stretch.

"Let me tell you a story that a good friend of mine, Mark, shared with me a few months ago," John said as we both took our seats.

"Great. I enjoy your stories," I responded.

"Mark told our men's group a story from his high school days. He and a friend started a house painting company. They hired several high school boys from their youth group at church. They had a practice of trying to finish early on Fridays so the group could go boating and skiing on a local lake," John began.

"They had just finished a large exterior painting job around noon on a Friday. The weather was perfect and the crew was eager to hit the lake. It was Mark's custom to walk around the house with the client to make sure they were happy with the work. Mark did just that and the client gave them their check," John said.

"That sounds fine. What happened next?" I asked, getting into his story.

"As Mark was finishing the walk with the customer, he remembered something he had seen earlier. While on the roof of the house, Mark noticed that the back side of the chimney had not received the final coat of paint. It was in an area no one would ever see," John explained, telling the story as if he had been there.

"So, what did he do?" I asked, seeing the connection to my current situation.

"Mark stood in the driveway as he looked at the chimney, and then looked at his friends who were anxious to head to the lake. Mark was driving the same kind of car you had, a Chevy Chevette. It was loaded down with paint, tarps and brushes and a couple of ladders were strapped down to the roof. Loading this car at the end of a job was no small task," John painted the picture.

"It was about then that Mark remembered something from that morning. They had a practice of starting each day with one of the team leading a short devotional. That very morning the scripture they had discussed was Colossians 3:23.

'Whatever you do, do your work heartily, as for the Lord, rather than for men.'"

"Mark went over to his team and told them the situation and his decision. They took out the ladder and materials needed to finish the job," John concluded.

"I guess what you are saying is that I now report to a higher authority," I said.

"You are right. You need to do your work to such a high standard that you would be proud if Jesus, Himself, was checking your work. Mark knew no earthly person would have ever known the difference, but he knew he would not have been able to sleep that night if he had taken that short cut," John added.

"That is a high standard!" I exclaimed.

"The neat thing is if you do your work with that in mind, your customers will be the ones who benefit. Over time, they will see the difference between you and other companies and recognize that they can trust you. It may even open up an opportunity for you to share with your clients and employees why you have such a high standard," John commented. "That's when your work takes on an eternal perspective."

"I can think of another advantage to creating that kind of culture," I added.

"What is that, Jim?" John asked.

"Not only will my customers benefit from a high level of service, but I will be able to count on my employees to do the right thing when no one is watching," I replied.

"That is very true. It is nice to be able to trust your workers. You have to know that not all of your employees will come under the leadership of Jesus, and even those who do are not perfect. Even Christians who have a solid relationship with Jesus make mistakes," John cautioned.

"This is true. But at least I can hold that up as a goal and encourage people to adopt a higher standard of integrity in the way we conduct our business," I said.

"If you ever want me to come back and speak to your leadership team or employees, I would be happy to do so. At my age, I can get away with speaking a challenging word," John offered.

"Thanks for the offer. I like that idea. Why don't we plan for you to talk to my leaders some Monday morning? They would enjoy seeing you again," I commented.

"Sounds great," John said, excited to be invited back.

"Well, I will tackle the billing issue this week and wait on the Lord to point out the next area where He wants me to raise the bar," I stated.

"Good plan. I'll wait to hear how you deal with that one. Why don't you summarize what we talked about today?" John asked.

"I'll give it a shot," I replied, turning back a page in my notebook.

July 19 – Meeting with John

♦ *I am now supposed to do my work as though Jesus is watching and approving everything I do.*

♦ *I am responsible for correcting mistakes with my customers, even if it is uncomfortable.*

♦ *Our customers will benefit when we conduct our business with integrity.*

"I had better hit the road. Cheri will be waiting. Tell Sallie hello for me. We will have to take the two of you out for dinner to thank you for all this great advice," I suggested.

"That would be fun. Remember, you get what you pay for, but as long as you look to God's Word to confirm what I say, you should be in pretty good shape," John laughed. "Oh, I forgot that I need to take next Friday off. Sallie and I are going out of town to visit some friends."

"That is fine. Then I will see you two weeks from Monday at our leadership team meeting," I said as I left and headed for home.

I told Cheri about my discussion with John and bounced my idea by her about correcting things with the clients we had overcharged.

Saturday morning, I was up again at an early hour to spend some extended time in prayer. I truly wanted to do what was right, but I needed help in creating my plan. I reread the verses

John pointed out during our meeting. It seemed pretty clear to me that I had to correct this wrong.

I drafted a letter to be sent along with an accompanying check to any client that had been overcharged. I knew I might lose some clients by being honest with them, but I hoped they would give us another chance to provide quality services.

I arrived at the office early on Monday morning, wanting to explain this plan to the leadership team and gain their buy in. The team all arrived on time and I shared what we were going to do. Asking the accounting team to review the time sheets and client bills for the past two years to identify anything that looked suspicious as the first step. They would then do some research and calculate the amount we had overcharged the client. A personal letter of apology from me along with the check would then be mailed to each affected client.

"What do you think?" I asked, wanting to see who was really on board with this new standard of conduct.

"I think it is the right thing to do," Jeff chimed in. "But where is the money going to come from? Do we each have to take it out of our budgets?"

"I expected that question and have decided we will utilize our reserve fund to handle this. It was not the fault of any one of you, but a result of a corporate culture that encouraged this behavior," I responded, setting their minds at ease.

"I do want each of you to communicate what we are doing to your teams. They need to know, as of today, that type of dishonesty is no longer acceptable at S & J Systems," I added.

"I want our customers to know we will always provide a high quality of service for a fair price."

"We will shoot to have the letters ready to mail next week," I said.

"There is one more item on the agenda before we start our day. I want every leader to take a look at your area and identify if there are any more issues like this hiding. We will take some time next Monday to discuss anything you find," I concluded.

The next few days, I waited anxiously for the report from the accounting department. My accounts receivable manager stopped by on Thursday afternoon to give me the news. Fortunately, it was not as widespread as I had first thought. There were a handful of clients and a few of our teams that accounted for most of the problems.

I was feeling good about our new direction. With John's help, I felt we were going to turn this ship around. The best part of it was that I already had the opportunity to share what prompted this change with three employees. They noticed a change in attitude within the leadership and stopped by to discuss it with me. I was able to tell them about my new relationship with Jesus and the changes He was making in my life. They all listened intently and one even wanted to know how she could experience the same thing in her life.

John was right. That meant more to me than closing the largest of business deals. Things had really changed in just a short time.

I missed spending Friday afternoon with John and looked forward to catching up the next week.

Chapter 10

IT TAKES A TEAM

Monday was a rainy day and I really missed my front row parking place. I had to stop by the kids' school before heading to the office, so I had to park further away from the door than I had ever done before. Even though my shoes were soaked by the time I reached my office, I felt good about the change in our policy. Several of the longtime employees were running through the parking lot with me, and I could tell they were surprised to see me when we put our umbrellas down together.

It was quite a sight to see: The entire leadership team arrived in my office right on time, and it was obvious everyone had made a similar jog through the rain. I expected some of them to be resentful of the fact that I had taken away their front row parking, but not a single person complained.

I started the meeting by going around the room to get an update from each department head. It was then that I noticed something for the first time. As each person began their update, I observed the body language of the rest of the team. Although everyone was polite and listened, they all pushed back from the table when it was not their turn to speak. When Jeff shared some of his challenges in the help desk area, the group sat quietly and no one offered any suggestions or assistance.

I made a note to discuss this with John on Friday.

Something else bothered me that morning. Even though I was aware of this, it had never seemed strange to me that my leadership team was 100% male. I knew we had many very capable female leaders in the company, but they had never been promoted to the executive level.

"And, by the way, I have invited John to come talk with our team next week," I announced.

The rest of the meeting went well and the group was dismissed to go tackle the challenges in their areas. Jenny, who had been my dad's executive assistant and was now my assistant, was as close to family as you could be without being blood related. She had been with S & J Systems since just about its beginning. If we were going to write a book about the company, she would be the first person I would call.

"Jenny, how are you doing this morning?" I asked.

"Great Mr. Wilson," she replied. "How are you?"

"Jenny, how many times do I have to tell you that you can call me Jim?" I laughed.

"I know. I guess long habits are hard to break," she responded. My dad had always maintained a very formal relationship with his assistant.

"Do you have a few minutes?" I asked. "I have something I need to get your advice on."

Jenny gave me a funny look and replied, "Sure. What's on your mind?"

Jenny had been very quiet for the past few weeks as I had been implementing some of the changes. I was eager to get her opinion on a lot of things, but today I had one topic in mind.

Jenny joined me in my office. I had made it a practice to always leave the door open when I was alone with a female. Even before becoming a Christian, I had heard about Billy Graham having that policy in order to avoid any appearance of wrong.

"Jenny, you have been around here forever. Why are there no females on the executive team? I know we have many qualified people, but they don't seem to have ever made it to this floor," I commented.

I could tell Jenny was a bit uncomfortable with this question. "Jenny, please speak your mind. I wouldn't have asked if I didn't want your honest opinion."

"Well Jim, I think it goes back to your father. He was a great man, don't get me wrong, but he had some beliefs and practices with which I did not always agree. How can I put this?" Jenny started slowly.

"Go ahead, tell me what you're thinking," I urged.

"Deep down, I don't think your father felt that a woman was capable of holding a senior leadership position. He didn't think they could be 'tough' enough to get the job done. He always treated me well, but I overheard many conversations where he degraded female employees," Jenny continued.

"That is what I guessed. I'm sorry, but I never realized it was an issue until this morning. I guess I picked up more of my dad's habits than I realized," I said.

"That's OK Jim. I had a feeling this day would come. I have been watching the change in you and how you have carried those changes out in our company. I think you are doing a great job," Jenny responded with an encouraging tone.

"Thanks Jenny. I have to admit, I am more excited about my future and that of our company than I have ever been," I said. "I have one more request for you."

"What is it?" Jenny asked.

"I would like to have your honest opinion on those female members of our team who have been overlooked for promotions. I don't want to promote someone just to make a point, but I'm sure we have some highly qualified candidates who could really add value up here. Please think about it and let me know if anyone comes to mind."

"I will put some serious thought into that. Thanks for asking for my opinion, Jim. It means a lot."

"Sure. You know how important you are to me. Not just for your work here, but your support of my family and the friend you have become to my mother," I said.

I was tempted to give John a call, and it was only Monday; but I held off and added this to my list of topics for Friday.

We were ahead of schedule in dealing with our overcharging problem. The letters were signed and ready to go out to the affected clients, along with the checks for the amount we had overcharged them plus 10%. I have to admit, I was a bit nervous to hear the response from our clients who had trusted us for so long. I took some time that afternoon to call some of our largest clients who would be receiving letters.

The rest of the week went by quickly. Overall, the response was positive from our clients who received their checks and letters. We had a couple of clients who went back and reviewed their bills, looking for other errors now that their confidence had been shaken in our company.

I arrived at the ballpark a half hour early. Cheri was attending a luncheon for one of her friends, so we had to skip lunch this week. John pulled up just as I was getting out of my car.

"Good timing!" I hollered as he approached.

"You are a bit early, Jim. You must have a lot on your mind," John said. He gave me a bear hug.

"I do. Thanks again for giving this time to me every week. I don't know if I could have made this adjustment without your help," I said as we walked through the gate. "I missed meeting with you last week. Did you and Sallie have a nice trip?"

"Yes. It was very relaxing. I think Sallie has already booked a return trip!" John replied.

"I brought a treat for us today. Cheri made one of her fruit pizzas for us," I said. John immediately went for two plates from the kitchen.

"Let's sit at the table for a change today," John suggested.

"Sounds fine to me."

"So, what do you want to talk about today?" John asked.

"First of all, I want to tell you about our solution to the billing errors. We reviewed our last two years worth of bills and found a handful of clients whom we had incorrectly charged. Here is a copy of the letter we sent. We mailed this letter along with a check for the amount of the error plus 10%," I said.

"Did you hear from any of your clients?" John asked.

"Yes. Most of them appreciated our honesty, even if it was a bit late. The best news was some of my employees are starting to notice the change. I had the opportunity to share about my relationship with Christ with another employee this week. Do you remember Laura in the accounting department?"

"Sure. I always liked her. Was she the one you shared with?" John asked.

"Yes. She has never been to church and has been very skeptical of Christians. She said she sensed a real change in the way the company was being run and wanted to find out what was behind it," I explained.

"That's what it's all about! The services S & J Systems offers our clients allows us to provide for our families, but ultimately, it is the place where we can exercise our faith to make a difference in the lives of others." John exclaimed, obviously excited to see changes being noticed.

"Well, we had better get started. I have a lot to ask you about and I only have you for three hours," I said.

"I'm all yours. Go ahead!" John said as we took a big bite of the dessert.

I told John about what I had observed in my leadership team meeting this week.

"They just don't seem to care about anything except what happens in their own department. I have also noticed there are a couple of leaders who give the appearance they think their department is more important than the others. I bet you can guess who I'm talking about," I started.

"Let me guess. Could you be speaking about the network consulting group?" John asked with a smile.

"You got it. They tend to be our most highly educated employees and they bill out at a very high rate. They think the rest of the company exists to support them," I continued.

"Do you have any ideas on how I can get them to all work more as a team?" I asked.

John got up from the table and retrieved his Bible.

"Somehow I knew you were going to start with God's Word. I hope I get to the point in my faith where I turn there first instead of having to wait for you to point me in the right direction," I commented.

John turned to 1 Corinthians 12 and started reading at verse 12. I had heard these verses before but never related them to my work. He read through verse 26 and then gave me his thoughts in this area.

"This part of the Word tells me that everyone is important and we each have a unique role to play. For all of us to be successful, each person has to do his or her part. If you have a weak billing department, it won't matter how brilliant your consultants are if you don't receive payment for what they do," John explained.

"This is what you were talking about several weeks ago when you told me that my role as a leader does not make me any better than people filling other roles in the company," I added.

"I'm glad you were listening!" John said smiling. "That is exactly right. When every group starts to appreciate what the other groups do, everyone benefits, including your customers," John continued. "And, as you noticed in your meeting, it all starts at the top."

"Your goal as a leader is to identify each employee's strengths and weaknesses and then put them in a job where they can be successful. I call it 'getting the right people doing the right things,'" John added.

"I have another issue. What can I do to get my leadership team to start working together?" I asked, not having a clue where to start with the problem.

"The first thing you need to do is let them know you expect them as leaders in this company to be knowledgeable about each part of the company. You can help by assigning them to cross functional teams to address your most pressing issues in the company," John suggested.

"I have a couple of things in mind. I will think about that and act on it Monday morning," I replied. The wheels were starting to turn.

John continued, "If you work with your leadership team on this and challenge them to learn an area outside of their expertise, you will start to see a change. You will know you have arrived if an outsider attends your leadership team meeting and has a tough time telling who is responsible for a particular area. Your goal is for every leader to be eager to assist the other teammates in solving problems in their areas."

"Makes sense. I will think about how to challenge the team during one of our leadership team meetings," I replied.

"If you would like, I can address this topic when I come meet with the team on Monday," John offered.

"That would be great," I acknowledged.

"You also need to impress upon every employee, from the receptionist to your most technical consultant, that they are all the face of S & J Systems when interacting with potential or existing clients," John said as he leaned forward and continued.

"I was at a business the other day and had a problem with the service delivery," John started.

I knew him well enough to know he was being very kind in his telling of the story. John was not one to put up with poor customer service.

"The person behind the counter was not interested in solving the problem, and then she uttered the words that made me cringe, 'I just work here,'" John said pushing back from the table.

"You must educate each employee concerning the basics of what S & J Systems is about and what services you offer your clients. They also need to know how to deal with a problem and whom to call if it is over their head. They should never respond with those words," John passionately said.

"I can tell this is a pet area of yours," I observed.

"Yes it is and I could go on forever, but I know you have other things on your mind," John responded. He calmed down and took the last bite of his dessert.

"I need your help explaining some of the history behind this next problem," I said. "It really bothered me when I realized there is not a single female member on our executive team."

"I knew this topic would come up eventually. I don't want to pass the buck on this one, but your dad had a real problem with placing women in leadership roles. My fault was not being strong enough to stand up to him on this issue," John said. He was obviously not proud of his record in this area.

"Let me beat you to it," I said. "What does God's Word have to say about this?"

"You are learning something!" John laughed. He again opened his Bible.

"Many people today misinterpret what the Bible has to say about this topic. Jesus was actually one of the first public leaders to show women respect," John replied and then read the story of the woman at the well found in John 4:1-30.

"I have heard that story for years, but what does it have to do with hiring a woman as an executive?" I questioned.

"I read that story because it shows Jesus was ahead of His time in treating women equally. It was not common during those days for a man to even speak to a woman in public. Jesus had an extended conversation with her and reached out to her point of need," John answered.

"There are other examples in the Bible where Jesus respected women. I honestly feel having some female influence on the leadership team would be a great addition. Men and women do not always think the same way, and for years, S & J Systems has been denied the benefit of a different perspective," John surmised.

"I would have to agree. After I noticed this problem, I talked with Jenny. She is going to help me correct the situation. My goal is to find a qualified female leader and immediately promote her to the executive team. From now on, I want to consider any candidate for promotion based on their merits, not their sex," I explained my plan to John.

"I agree with your approach. Your workforce is made up of almost 50% females. You will be amazed at how energized they will become when they have an equal opportunity to excel and contribute in the company," John added.

"Is there anything else?" John asked.

"My mind is really spinning, but I think I've got enough to chew on for this week," I replied, standing to take the dishes to the kitchen.

"Not so quick!" John laughed. "Why don't you wrap up our session by summarizing what you have learned?"

I sat back down and smiled, "I thought I would get out of here easy today, but I can't pull that by you."

I flipped back a few pages and read my notes as John listened and added a few points.

August 2 – Meeting with John

- We will be more effective as a leadership team if everyone has a sincere interest in every part of the company.
- One way to encourage teamwork is to assign people to solve a problem that involves more than their area.
- One of the goals of every leader should be to get the right people doing the right things, matching employees with their talents.
- Every employee must know the basics of the products and services sold by our company.
- "I just work here" should be a forbidden phrase!
- Having a diverse leadership team, including females, will provide better solutions to your challenges.
- Jesus was one of the first public leaders to show respect to women.

"Am I dismissed now?" I said with a smirk.

"You are. This was a good discussion today, Jim. In some ways, I feel I am able to work through you to correct some of the problems I was responsible for during my time at S & J," John said.

"Your help is invaluable, John. I sure am glad you went to that conference," I said. I shook his hand and headed out the door.

"Hold on. I'll walk out with you. Sallie and I are going on a date tonight," John commented as we both made our way to our cars.

"I'll see you on Monday morning," John said.

"That's right. We start promptly at 8:00 a.m., so why don't you stop by a few minutes early so we can grab a cup of coffee?" I suggested.

"See you then. Have a great weekend," John replied.

Chapter 11

FAITHFUL IN THE SMALL THINGS

On Saturday morning, I gave Jenny a call at home to see if she had any thoughts on my female executive decision. She gave me her advice. I was happy to see we were both thinking in the same direction. Donna Harris had been a leader in our sales and marketing department and had been the one to come up with many of our successful programs. I don't exactly know why, but we had never included that department on the executive team.

I gave Donna a call and arranged to meet her for coffee that afternoon. She had no idea why I had arranged the meeting, and she seemed a bit nervous when I started our conversation. I told her I had observed her excellent leadership and the outstanding results from her department for several years. She almost fell out of her chair when I said that I wanted her to join the executive team.

The weekend went by quickly, and before I knew it, Monday morning had arrived. I got up extra early and had a great time of reading and prayer. I don't always like getting out of bed to have my personal time with the Lord each morning, but I can really tell a difference in my days since I began this habit. On the occasional morning when I missed this time, I realized I did not handle situations properly and said things that I wished I could take back.

I stopped by the local bakery and picked up some kolaches and donuts for our leadership team meeting. Food always improved the quality of our meetings!

The company was showing some signs of new life and we had picked up two new large accounts in the past two weeks. For the first time in several years, I did not spend a significant portion of my week dealing with critical personnel shortages. We were doing a lot of things right.

"Morning, Jim!" John exclaimed as he got off the elevator and headed for my office.

"Hello, John. Great to see you. Thanks for getting up early and interrupting your busy schedule to come meet with us," I returned.

"No problem. It sure feels funny coming back here at this hour of the morning. I'm glad it is just for a visit," John chuckled.

"Can I get you some coffee?" I asked.

"Sure. Are you still using that same coffee vendor?" John inquired.

"Yes, but they have started offering all those fancy flavors and they aren't half bad," I answered.

John and I sat in my office and shared stories from the weekend and prepared for the leadership team to arrive.

"I know the team will be excited to see you. If you want, you can take a few minutes and update them on what has been going on in your life since you left," I suggested.

The team started to arrive and exchanged friendly greetings with John. John had always been the warmer, more compassionate half of the partnership.

"Wow, John. You must be special if the boss sprung for donuts!" Jeff joked after seeing the spread on the conference table. "We need you to come back every week!"

The team settled into their normal seats, and we began the meeting. I introduced our topic of the morning and let the team know that I had invited John to share his thoughts on how we could become a more effective leadership team.

"Before John begins, I want to introduce the newest member of our executive team. All of you know Donna and are aware of the great work she has done for years. I think it makes sense to have the sales and marketing department represented on this team," I announced to the all-male team.

"Welcome, Donna!" Jeff was the first to stand and shake her hand. "It will be great to have your ideas in these meetings."

The rest of the team echoed Jeff's sentiments, and I could tell Donna felt at home in her new role.

"Now, back to our topic of the morning. John, the floor is yours," I said. I grabbed a chocolate covered donut and took my seat.

John did an excellent job of talking to the team about how critical it is for everyone to work together to serve our customers. He challenged the leadership team members to partner up with another team member and spend some time learning about their area, including the challenges they face.

"Do any of you have any questions for me?" John offered as he concluded his comments.

"I have one for you," Jeff jumped at the opportunity.

"Go ahead," John motioned.

"For several years, we have had a relationship with another high-tech consulting company. We found that we were losing some big contracts because we were lacking some skills on the high end of our business. The leadership team had made the decision that this labor class was too high priced to keep on the payroll for the occasional job that required their expertise," Jeff began.

"How has that relationship been working?" John probed.

"Up until four months ago, very well," Jeff replied. "It was about the same time that I began to receive some complaints from several of our key clients. I noticed these unhappy clients had one thing in common. They all had projects that used our outsourcing partner."

"I know where this is going," John interrupted.

"Do you have any advice on how to handle this situation?" Jeff asked.

John looked at me to make sure I was fine with him addressing this issue. I motioned for him to proceed. I had known John long enough to know that anything he said would be consistent with my thoughts.

"That is a challenging dilemma. Sometimes it makes financial sense to form partnerships like that to be able to meet the needs of your clients. In reality, the clients are usually unaware that these additional consultants are not directly on your payroll. The actions and behaviors of these outsourced consultants reflect on the reputation of S & J Systems," John began.

"So, how do I make this relationship work for us and the client?" Jeff questioned.

"Even though these individuals work for another company, if they are going to represent you with one of your clients, they need to understand the expectations you have in regard to customer service and quality issues. It would be a good idea for you to include them in an orientation program along with some of your new team members," John answered.

"And, one more thing. You must ensure they are accountable for their work and behaviors. If their company does not have someone on-site to supervise them, then you must establish a process with the company to provide regular performance feedback for their employees," John added.

"That makes sense. I will think about what you have said and call a meeting with the head of this outsourced company," Jeff responded.

We wrapped up the leadership team meeting, and I walked John out to his car.

"Thanks for being here today, John," I said. "I was watching the team as you were talking and they seemed to be embracing what you were saying. I will follow up with them later this week to see how they are doing on selecting a partner."

"I enjoyed being here. I think you have the beginning of a solid leadership team. There is a part of me that wished I could be involved in this transformation," John responded.

"You could always come back," I offered.

"I said there was a 'part' of me that wished it. I did not mention that it was a very small part," John laughed. "I am enjoying my retirement and spending time with Sallie."

"I understand. I have a few more years before I can even think about that," I said as John got in his car.

"See you on Friday," John waved. He closed the door and zoomed out of the parking lot.

I returned to my office and was immediately jerked back to reality with a whole slew of problems to tackle. Just when I felt things were going in the right direction, I took a few small steps backward.

The rest of the week was the same. We had some victories, and then some setbacks. I was ready for my visit with John by the time Friday rolled along. We had both agreed we would make this the last scheduled meeting for a while. I needed some time to work on what we had discussed and John was going to take an extended vacation.

John called the night before and told me to wear shorts and a T-shirt to our meeting. I tried to find out what he was scheming, but he was determined to keep it a secret.

When I pulled into the parking lot at Wranglers stadium, John was waiting with Mike at the gate.

"What are you up to?" I asked John as he gave me a smile.

"Mike and I have a surprise for you," John replied.

Instead of heading up to John's suite, we walked down toward the field.

Mike let me in on the secret, "John told me that you used to be quite a baseball player yourself in college. I have arranged for you to join the team for batting practice today."

I was excited but a bit nervous. I had not swung a bat in 10 years, and these guys were all out of my league.

I talked the pitcher into giving me some easy pitches and was able to connect with a few of them. It didn't take long before I was out of breath and my hands were hurting.

"That's enough for me! I'm glad I don't have to face you throwing your hard stuff," I said to the pitcher.

"Thanks, guys!" I said to the players as we wrapped up my turn. "Good luck on the game tonight."

John, Mike and I headed up to the suite. John had invited Mike to join us for this meeting.

"Mike, I've been meaning to let you know what a great job your staff does out here. We have been to a few games this year, and I am constantly amazed at the level of excellent service we receive. It is not something I had expected after attending many other ballparks in my lifetime," I said.

"Thanks for the encouragement. We do try hard to provide an exceptional experience for our guests," Mike replied.

We all grabbed a drink and settled into the seats on the balcony.

"What do you want to discuss for our last meeting?" John asked me.

"I have really appreciated getting together with you, John, and I feel we are making some definite progress at the office. My frustration comes from the time I spend each week dealing with insignificant things that blow up and result in an upset customer and a lot of wasted energy on our part," I tried to explain.

"John, do you mind if I take a stab at this one?" Mike asked.

"Go right ahead," John motioned.

"We dealt with that very situation at my last company. I realized we had developed a culture that ignored things until they demanded our attention. I had a great friend and mentor, Doug Henshaw, whom I went to see about this concern," Mike began.

John smiled, knowing this individual and the rest of the story.

"He had a saying that really made sense," Mike continued.

"What was that?" I asked.

"He said,

> 'If you make a big deal out of little things, then the little
> things won't become a big deal.'"

John jumped in, "I can't agree more. As you would expect, the Bible has something to say about this area."

I smiled and said, "I figured that would be our next stop in this discussion."

John had already grabbed his Bible before we had moved outside. "Let's take a look at the life of Joseph. I'm sure you remember how his brothers sold him into slavery because of their jealousy."

"Yes. That was always one of my favorite Bible stories growing up. Please continue," I said.

"Well, Joseph was faithful to perform his duties with excellence, even when they included things like cleaning the floor or serving others. He then spent years in prison because he had been falsely accused by the wife of Potiphar. Joseph continued to trust God. When he was released, he was given a position of authority. If he had not done a good job as a humble slave, he would not have been given the bigger opportunity," John concluded.

Mike jumped back in, (I felt like I was in a tag-team mentoring session.) "I have another scripture that relates to this area. Are you familiar with the parable of the talents?"

"I remember hearing it, but go ahead and refresh my memory," I replied.

"I will paraphrase it, but if you want to look it up later, you can find it in Matthew 25: 14-30," Mike began. "The story is about a master who was going to be out of town for awhile and he entrusted three of his workers with his money to watch and invest. Two of the workers were good stewards. They took the portion they were entrusted with and doubled the money through hard work. The last worker took and hid the money."

"I remember this now," I said. "Didn't the master come home and reward the two who had done something with the money and punished the one who did nothing?"

"You got it," Mike responded. "The implication for your work is that the Lord expects us to do a good job wherever you find yourself. This also means you should treat every client with respect, regardless of their size."

"I learned that lesson the hard way," I added. "I blew off a small client and our team did a poor job providing services for them. It wasn't until the next month I realized how foolish that was. The owner of the company was related to the owner of one of our largest clients. He canceled our service because of the way we treated his relative."

John concluded, "This also applies to small tasks, regardless of the size of the client. In the grand scheme of things, you may be providing excellent service, but you may lose a client by being careless on some things that seem insignificant to you but are a big deal to your client."

Mike added, "God expects you to be a good steward of what He has given you. That means when you are in a significant leadership position with hundreds of employees depending on you, He will expect much out of you. Try to make every decision, no matter how small, only after seeking the Lord's counsel."

"Wow. I am tired from my workout and all this discussion. Thanks for joining us today, Mike," I said.

"It was my pleasure. I'd better get going. We have a game starting in two hours," Mike said as he got up and headed out to make the pre-game rounds.

John and I cleaned up and took a seat back inside. "Why don't I summarize today's main points? You may have to fill in the gaps," I suggested.

"Go for it," John said, giving me his full attention.

Opening my notebook, I went over the main points, including some of my notes from our leadership team meeting earlier in the week.

August 9 – Meeting with John

♦ Make sure we are delivering quality services to every client, no matter how small they may be.

♦ Make a big deal out of the little things, so the little things won't become a big deal.

♦ Something may seem insignificant to us, but it may be very important to a client.

♦ God expects us to use the talents He has given us to the best of our ability.

♦ Joseph reached a position of importance only after doing a great job in his humble role as a servant.

"That was great," John said. "Why don't I conclude our last session by praying for you and the company?"

"I would appreciate that," I said. We both knelt and John voiced a sincere prayer.

"Amen," I added after John finished.

"I'd better be on my way. Cheri has something going on and I need to get home. I don't know what it is, but she told me not to schedule anything else tonight."

"I will give you a call when we get back from vacation. I would like to continue meeting with you now and then. I enjoy your company," John said as I headed for the door.

Chapter 12

EXTRA INNINGS

I walked out the door and around the corner and found several people I knew.

"Hi Daddy!" both kids yelled as they ran into my arms.

Cheri and Sallie were also both there.

"We decided to surprise you and come join you for a game," Cheri said with a grin.

John walked around the corner smiling and said, "I thought it would be fun to have our families see the ball game after our last session."

Cheri planned ahead as usual and brought a change of clothes. "I thought you might want these after your minor league baseball debut."

Obviously, Cheri and John had arranged this evening without my knowledge.

"Thanks. I think I will go in and change," I replied.

We all went into the suite and began what would be a fun evening with my family.

The service we received was outstanding. I thought this might be because we were in the suite. I was interested to see how the service was in the regular seats, so Cheri and I left the kids with John and Sallie and took a walk. Every employee at the ballpark was friendly and made eye contact with us if we looked in their direction.

There was a great variety of food options and special treats for the kids.

"So how was your last session with John?" Cheri asked as we began our lap around the field.

"It was excellent as usual. Mike joined us and tossed in his thoughts. We talked some more about teamwork, but spent most of the time discussing how important it is to do a good job in everything we attempt. This also includes the trivial or small items in life that we could easily ignore," I replied.

Just then a foul ball came heading our direction and landed in the section near where we were walking. A fan had unsuccessfully attempted to catch the ball and then it crashed into the seat behind him. Immediately, two employees of the park were there to make sure no one was hurt.

"That was close!" Cheri said with a sigh of relief.

"We had one almost hit me in the suite a couple of weeks ago," I added.

"Do you feel more prepared to lead S & J Systems?" Cheri asked.

"Yes, I do. John has given me a great gift. Not only did he show me how to have a relationship with Jesus, but he invested his time to make sure I was able to apply the truths found in the Bible to my challenges at work," I answered.

"It is amazing how a book written so long ago can be so relevant in our time," I added.

"I am also thankful for John," Cheri began. "Every aspect of our life has improved in the past few months. I no longer feel that we are living separate lives, one at work, one at church and a third at home."

"I agree. It is amazing how much peace I feel having turned every area of my life over to Jesus. Things aren't perfect and I still have challenges, especially at work, but I now have a resource and a person who can help me deal with life," I replied.

We continued our walk around the park and headed back up to the suite. The kids were enjoying eating the large variety of food and sitting out on the balcony.

The game was exciting and the Wranglers won in the last inning.

"We had better head for home and get these kids to bed," I said after the game ended.

"Thanks for coming and sharing the evening with us," John said graciously.

"No. Thank you for inviting us. It was quite a surprise and a great way to end the day," I replied.

Cheri gave John and Sallie a hug. "Thanks for everything. You will never realize the full impact you have made on Jim and our entire family."

"It has been my pleasure. When we return from vacation, I would like to continue meeting if Jim is interested," John replied.

"I can answer that right now. I will be waiting for your call," I said.

"Jim, I want to share one final verse with you before you leave," John said. "This summarizes how we should live. It is found in Matthew, chapter 6, verse 33.

> 'But seek first His kingdom and His righteousness, and all these things shall be added unto you.'"

"Make sure you stay consistent with having your prayer time each morning and reading God's Word. I will be excited to see the changes you are making at the company. Jim, your dad would be proud of the man you have become and the way you are handling the company."

"Thanks, John. See you soon."

We headed out to the parking lot. On our way out of the stadium, we had at least 10 employees sincerely thank us for coming to the game. They obviously have a good coach!

Many months went by and I continued to grow in my knowledge of the scripture and how it applies in every part of my life. John and I resumed our meetings but only on a monthly basis. There were several occasions for me to give him a call for advice on an issue in between our regular meetings.

Several months ago, I was alone on a Saturday morning. Cheri and the kids had gone to a friend's house to play for a few hours. My eyes caught the notebook I had used during my meetings with John. Picking it up and reading over my notes, I realized these truths were timeless. I decided to spend the morning summarizing the important points so they could quickly be reviewed every month to make sure I was still on track.

Following is the summary created that day. I hope it is as helpful to you as it has been for me. My prayer is that you will put these principles into practice in your own life and avoid making many of the mistakes I made in the early days of my career.

Biblical Life Principles According to John

- ◆ *We spend more time at work than in any other area of our life. If we have invited Jesus into our lives, it makes sense that we should include Him in our careers.*

- ◆ *The Bible is a very practical book and has a lot to say about the business world and topics like money, trials and honesty.*

- The "Golden Rule" is a great customer service model. I should think about every action and wonder if I would like to be treated that way.

- Prayer is an important tool. Jesus wants me to pray about my decisions at work.

- Jesus is a great model of leadership. He could have demanded the perks of His position, but He served others instead.

- Just because I am in a leadership position does not mean that I am smarter or better than people in other roles. That is the position God arranged for me.

- Leaders must be willing to jump in and help when needed, instead of thinking they are above any job.

- I need to lead by example in dealing with customers. My employees will follow my lead.

- Don't get discouraged. I don't have to change everything at once.

- I am now supposed to do my work as though Jesus is watching and approving everything I do.

- I am responsible for correcting mistakes with my customers, even if it is uncomfortable.

- Our customers will benefit when we conduct our business with integrity.

- We will be more effective as a leadership team if everyone has a sincere interest in every part of the company.

- One way to encourage teamwork is to assign people to solve a problem that involves more than their area.

- One of the goals of every leader should be to get the right people doing the right things, matching employees with their talents.
- Every employee must know the basics of the products and services sold by our company.
- "I just work here" should be a forbidden phrase!
- Having a diverse leadership team, including females, will provide better solutions to your challenges.
- Jesus was one of the first public leaders to show respect to women.
- Make sure we are delivering quality services to every client, no matter how small they may be.
- Make a big deal out of the little things, so the little things won't become a big deal.
- Something may seem insignificant to us, but it may be very important to a client.
- God expects us to use the talents He has given us to the best of our ability.
- Joseph reached a position of importance only after doing a great job in his humble role as a servant.

ABOUT THE AUTHOR

David Reed attended Texas A&M University where he received degrees in Chemical Engineering and Computer Science. Prior to founding Customer Centered Consulting Group, Inc., he served with Andersen Consulting, Exxon and Walt Disney World. David's mission is to utilize sound biblical principles to help organizations of all types and sizes improve their effectiveness by:

Getting the right *PEOPLE* (Human Resources) doing the

right *THINGS* (Operations) with the

right *ATTITUDE* (Customer Service) with the

right *TOOLS* (Technology) and for the

right *MONEY* (Finances).

David is also the author of an easy-read customer service book titled *Monday Morning Customer Service* and conducts customer service training and consulting for a variety of organizations.

David resides in Frisco, Texas with his wife and two children. He travels throughout the country, helping schools, churches, corporations and government agencies identify their strengths and weaknesses. Then, by working with leadership teams and teaching simple processes, he helps organizations create and implement common sense solutions to their problems.

Well-known as a speaker and trainer in corporate America, David has also been a featured guest and expert on programs and panels exploring various customer service issues.

MONDAY
MORNING
CUSTOMER SERVICE

It is always easier to learn from the experiences of others than to have to live through everything on your own. *Monday Morning Customer Service* allows you to do just that! This easy-read book follows Brett, a newly appointed director of guest services, as he meets with his mentor, Sam, for eight Monday mornings. During these sessions, Sam shares valuable lessons on topics from accountability to guest recovery. They discuss the difference of On Stage vs. Backstage and talk about scouting the competition. Brett begins this new chapter in his career armed with easy-to-implement ideas to transform his organization into one that is customer focused and successful.

Enjoy this easy-to-read customer service book also written by David Reed.

To order *Monday Morning Customer Service*, please visit us at www.cccginc.com.

Customer Centered
Consulting Group, Inc.

Customer Centered Consulting Group, Inc. was formed in 1999 to help organizations of all sizes improve their effectiveness through enhanced customer service, strong leadership and simple processes. With headquarters in Texas, the company's services are focused in the customer service area.

♦ Customer service assessments – Perform an objective review of your customer service as seen from the eye of a customer, client or partner. To perform this assessment, we utilize surveys, "mystery guest" observations, focus groups and a review of internal policies and procedures.

♦ Customer service training – Provide half-day and full-day interactive training sessions to refocus the attention on the customer and reinforce your policies and procedures that deal with the treatment of your customers.

♦ Customer feedback process creation – Create guest and customer surveys along with the internal process to put this information to work in your organization.

♦ Keynote addresses – Address your convention, conference, church group or internal meeting on topics of customer service and leadership.

In addition to the customer service area, Customer Centered Consulting Group, Inc. provides services in the human resources and business operations arenas.

Customer Centered Consulting Group Services

Customer Service Consulting & Speaking

- Customer service assessment
- Customer survey design
- Customer survey execution & analysis
- Keynote addresses
- Mystery shopper/mystery guest
- Focus group facilitation
- Training (half-day or full-day program)

Human Resources

- Executive coaching
- Personality profile exercise
- Recruiting process training
- Orientation training design
- Employee review process design
- Leadership training
- Mentoring program design
- Meeting facilitation
- Team building
- Retreat planning/facilitation
- Employee survey design
- Employee survey execution & analysis
- Time management training
- Facilitation skills training

Business Operations

- Annual "Game Plan" development
- Measurement program design
- Corporate structure/realignment
- Contingency planning
- Skills survey
- Help desk review/design
- Vision creation/communication

If you are interested in learning more about these services, please visit the website, call or send an email to info@cccginc.com

Customer Centered Consulting Group, Inc.
5729 Lebanon Dr., Suite 144-222
Frisco, TX 75034
(469) 633-9833 – voice
(469) 633-9843 – fax
www.cccginc.com

Customer Centered
Consulting Group, Inc.